The Destiny of Islam in the Endtimes

The Destiny of Islam in the Endtimes

UNDERSTANDING GOD'S HEART FOR THE MUSLIM PEOPLE

Faisal Malick

Previously published as *Here Comes Ishmael* Copyright © 2005 Faisal Malick by Guardian Books, an imprint of Essence Publishing, Ontario, Canada. Library and Archives Canada Cataloguing in Publication: ISBN 978-1-55306-943-0; BT1170.M28 2005; 261.2'7; C2005-902865-3.

DESTINY IMAGE® PUBLISHERS, INC.
P.O. Box 310, Shippensburg, PA 17257-0310

"Speaking to the Purposes of God for this Generation and for the Generations to Come."

This book and all other Destiny Image, Revival Press, Mercy Place, Fresh Bread, Destiny Image Fiction, and Treasure House books are available at Christian bookstores and distributors worldwide.

For a U.S. bookstore nearest you, call **1-800-722-6774.**

For more information on foreign distributors, call **717-532-3040.**

Or reach us on the Internet: **www.destinyimage.com.**

ISBN 10: 0-7684-2593-X

ISBN 13: 978-0-7684-2593-2

For Worldwide Distribution, Printed in the U.S.A.

1 2 3 4 5 6 7 8 9 10 11 / 09 08 07

Dedication

I dedicate this book to Ishmael and the 1.6 billion Muslim people he represents. You are not forgotten—you are chosen for such a time as this. This is your season to embrace the truth about your origin and your end-time destiny, planned before creation. Your cry will be heard, and you will behold the invisible in this hour.

> *I am sought of them that asked not for me; I am found of them that sought me not: I said Behold me, behold me, unto a nation that was not called by my name* (Isaiah 65:1).

Acknowledgments

I would like to thank my precious love and wife of substance, Sabina. You were the first to embrace the passion of this message and see the end from the beginning. You chose to stand in the gap for a misunderstood people and demonstrate the heart of Jesus. You have been an inspiration and encouragement to me throughout working on this book. I love you always. Without you even my destiny would be incomplete.

I would like to thank those of you who remain anonymous for your prayer and support for this book. You know who you are, and you are dear to my heart.

Acknowledgments

Endorsements

Faisal Malick has heard from Heaven about God's plan for Muslims. Christianity will change its world view of Islam!

—Sid Roth
Host, *It's Supernatural!*

Recently, the focus for worldwide prayer shifted to the Muslim world. For us to be effective in focusing in prayer, I had to ask the Lord to bring new contacts with new insight into our lives. My path was graced with Faisal Malick and the book, *The Destiny of Islam in the Endtimes.* This book will bring the best understanding of the concept of Islam, Ishmael, Esau, and terrorism. If you want to understand the most mysterious and misunderstood portion of the world, this book is a must read! *The Destiny of Islam in the Endtimes* brings a full comprehension of the Muslim cry that originated through the bondwoman, Hagar. This is a cry that says, "I need to be recognized, identified, and loved." This is a book that could change the course of the generation that is rising and affect the course of the world in this season.

—Chuck D. Pierce
Glory of Zion International Ministries, Inc., President
Global Harvest Ministries, Harvest Watchman

With amazing insight, Faisal Malick lifts our perspective higher into God's purposes in his timely book *The Destiny of Islam in the Endtimes.* Revelation flows...Scriptures unfold...and God's heart is revealed as you partake of the pages in your hands. The kairos time has come for the Islamic veil to be pierced and a great end-time harvest of souls to be welcomed in. This book will help pave the way!

—James W. Goll
Encounters Network

Faisal Malick's book not only brings amazingly clear understanding into the dynamics of Islam, but it also imparts a burden into the heart of the reader, as well as a love for the Muslim people. You will experience a major paradigm shift in your view of this precious people, and possibly conviction and repentance, as you see them through the eyes of God's destiny for them.

—Steve Shultz
Founder, The ElijahList,
ElijahRain Magazine, and Prophetic TV

The Western mind, for the most part, does not comprehend the vast world of Muslim thought, or the history of Islam. Faisal Malick has with great skill, love, and compassion, opened to us the inner workings of this world of thought and religion. From the genesis of Islam to present Muslim thought, Faisal writes so all can understand God's love for all humanity and desire to connect these dear people with the Lord Jesus Christ.

This book has helped me set aside preconceived judgments and realize that Muslims are a people hungry for truth, love, and understanding.

—Rev. Norm Maclaren
Vice President, Ministry
Crossroads Christian Communications

The Destiny of Islam in the Endtimes rocked my world when I read it. The book is full of revelatory insight from the Father's heart regarding the largest unreached people group in the world today. Faisal Malick helps us gain understanding, increase in love, and answer the call to action.

—Patricia King
Extreme Prophetic
www.extremeprophetic.com

Terrorists! Muslims! Arabs! For many in the Christian world these three groups are all thrown into one set—enemies to be avoided. But to the God of Heaven who loves the world and sent His Son to die for all, these are people to be loved. As you read this book, be prepared to also receive a call from the Lord to do something. The Lord has been speaking to me about the Muslim people from many sources, including dreams and prophetic words. When I read this book, my heart leapt with joy because I gained clarity about God's plan to reach the whole world. And I now know that I have a part to play in this drama of the endtimes—and I intend to fulfill it. My life was deeply impacted by Faisal Malick's work *The Destiny of Islam in the Endtimes.*

—Rich Marshall
Author, *God@Work* and *God@Work Volume 2*

The Destiny of Islam in the Endtimes helped me to differentiate between "radical Islam" and the descendants of Ishmael. Faisal Malick brings hope to any Christian who has deemed the Muslim people too difficult to reach with the Gospel. His testimony is exciting, his faith inspirational, and his vision revolutionary. *The Destiny of Islam* has renewed my burden and love for all of Abraham's children. I highly recommend this book.

—Dr. Ron Burgio
President, Elim Fellowship
Sr. Pastor, Love Joy Gospel Church

Written by a Muslim-turned-Christian, this book is more than it seems on the surface. It touches a nerve in the corporate heart of both Christianity and Islam. It is a sobering look at what will certainly be a growing concern in the days ahead. It requires the Church that Jesus is building to become all God intends her to be so she might accomplish all God intends her to do. Our only hope is a heart fixed on Jesus and discernment resting in His Spirit. This book is absolutely essential reading for the serious believer.

—Don Nori, Sr.
Publisher
Destiny Image Publishers

Table of Contents

Preface

THE primary intent of this book is to define and clarify the current season and create awareness of the significance of Ishmael in our times. I pray that we see beyond the lenses of our limitations into the counsel of God.

This book is not just about God's mercy in reaching out to the Muslim world but the statement that God is making to Israel, the Church, and the nations of the earth in showing His mercy, love, and compassion to the Muslim people. As you read, I pray that you recognize the statement God is making to you, and that you will look into the fullness of His all-encompassing purpose.

I write not just about the endtimes but more about the intent of God before the beginning of time. This is a message to the Muslim people; but if we are not careful, we may miss the message to us. I believe you will recognize that what God started in time, He already finished in eternity.

For me this is not just a message I am sharing with you—but a message that I am.

***Kairos** time is a moment when a portal is opened between time and eternity so an event can take place in its fullness, as appointed by God, to forever change the destiny of all people.*

Chapter 1

Who Is Ishmael?

TODAY 1.6 billion[1] Muslims stand at center stage, while the world watches and wonders. Israel warns of terrorism, the Church is watching the clock, and the people of Islam are seeking a revolution.

Simultaneously, a portal is opening between time and eternity over the Muslim world, making way for a *kairos moment* to occur. Humanity is responding to the season we are living in; not just any season, but the kairos moment for the Muslim people.

In the Greek language, time is divided into *chronos* and *kairos*. *Chronos* is chronological time, measured in seconds, minutes, days, and years. *Kairos* time is a moment when a portal is opened between time and eternity so an event can take place in its fullness, as appointed by God, to forever change the destiny of all people.

We know time as chronos and measure it. God knows time as kairos and destines it. A kairos moment opens the door to destiny, when that which has been hidden for ages is revealed. As the Church of Jesus Christ, we must discern kairos moments so we can flow with God. This chapter discusses the biblical origins of the Muslim people, the nature of their cry, and the heartbeat of God for this hour.

Biblical Origin of Muslims

Muhammad, the prophet of Islam, was a direct descendent of Ishmael through his second son, Kedar. Muhammad received revelations from an angel whom he believed to be Gabriel. These revelations later became the book of the Muslims, known as the Qur'an. Muslims believe that Abraham took his firstborn, Ishmael, to the altar of sacrifice on the mount instead of Isaac to substantiate Ishmael as the seed through which the whole earth would be blessed. The Muslims also believe that Muhammad was the fulfillment of God's promise to Abraham and that Muhammad was the prophet like unto Moses. They consider the Bible to be changed and not entirely authentic. The nation of Islam comes forth from Ishmael's descendent, Muhammad. So Islam's roots trace back to Ishmael, Abraham's first son.

Muslims believe Abraham took Ishmael to the altar of sacrifice—not Isaac.

Later Ishmael married an Egyptian and his family vastly expanded through 12 sons, leading to a multitude of people. The

Muslim people existed long before they embraced Islam. I have come to understand that God always looks at the root of an issue rather than merely at the surface.

While the servant of Abraham's wife, Hagar, was with child, the angel of the Lord found her in the wilderness and began to unveil God's plan:

> *And the angel of the Lord found her by a fountain of water in the wilderness, by the fountain in the way to Shur. And he said, Hagar, Sarai's maid, whence camest thou? and whither wilt thou go? And she said, I flee from the face of my mistress Sarai. And the angel of the Lord said unto her, Return to thy mistress, and submit thyself under her hands. And the angel of the Lord said unto her, I will multiply thy seed exceedingly, that it shall not be numbered for multitude* (Genesis 16:7-10).

God Named Ishmael Before Birth

Ishmael was the first person to ever be named by God before birth in all the earth. When something happens for the first time in the Bible, it is very significant and sets a precedent. It is called the law of first things. In the entire Bible, there are only four people whom God named before they were born through a divinely granted appearance of an angel or of Himself. There are others about whom God prophesied, but only four were named before birth in this divine way.

The first time something happens in the Bible, it sets a precedent.

The first was Ishmael, second was Isaac, third was John the Baptist, and the last was Jesus. (See Genesis 16:11, Genesis 17:19, Luke 1:13, Luke 1:31.) The Church knows the last three, but the first the Church has not seen.

> *And the angel of the LORD said unto her, Behold, thou art with child, and shalt bear a son, and shalt call his name Ishmael; because the LORD hath heard thy affliction* (Genesis 16:11).

Hagar went back to Sarai, as instructed by the angel of the Lord, and Ishmael was born. When Ishmael was about 13 years of age, God appeared to Abram and changed his name to Abraham and Sarai's name to Sarah (see Gen. 17:5 and Gen. 17:15). God discussed His covenant with Abraham and promised to give him and Sarah a son. Abraham beseeched the Lord about Ishmael, and God responded:

> *And Abraham said unto God, O that Ishmael might live before thee! And God said, Sarah thy wife shall bear thee a son indeed; and thou shalt call his name Isaac: and I will establish my covenant with him for an everlasting covenant, and with his seed after him. And as for Ishmael, I have heard thee: Behold, I have blessed him, and will*

make him fruitful, and will multiply him exceedingly; twelve princes shall he beget, and I will make him a great nation. But my covenant will I establish with Isaac, which Sarah shall bear unto thee at this set time in the next year (Genesis 17:18-21).

God blessed Ishmael and promised he would be exceedingly multiplied beyond number, with 12 princes, and would become a great nation. In Genesis 16:11, God named Ishmael before he was born, and in Genesis 17:20, God blessed Ishmael but established His covenant with Isaac, the promised seed. (More detailed discussion about why God blessed Ishmael is found in a following chapter.) Upon the weaning of Isaac, Sarah found Ishmael mocking Isaac and desired that the son of the bondwoman be cast out and not be an heir with her son, Isaac (see Genesis 21:9).

Abraham was grieved, like any father would be, and went to the Lord. God made it clear to him that in Isaac God's covenant would be established and in Isaac would his seed be called. As for Ishmael, he was to be cast out, but God confirmed again to Abraham that Ishmael would become a great nation. Ishmael, along with Hagar, was cast out of his father's house with no more than a little bread and water.

Wherefore she said unto Abraham, Cast out this bondwoman and her son: for the son of this bondwoman shall not be heir with my son, even with Isaac. And the thing was very grievous in Abraham's sight because of his son. And God said unto Abraham, Let it not be grievous in thy sight because of the lad, and because of thy bondwoman; in all that Sarah hath said unto thee, hearken unto her voice; for in Isaac shall thy seed be called. And also of the son of the bondwoman will I make a nation, because he is thy seed. And Abraham rose up early in the morning, and took bread, and a bottle of water, and gave it unto Hagar, putting it on her shoulder, and the child, and sent her away: and she departed, and wandered in the wilderness of Beersheba (Genesis 21:10-14).

The Supernatural Well

Ishmael, around the age of 15, was cast out with Hagar into the wilderness. Let's see what happens:

And the water was spent in the bottle, and she cast the child under one of the shrubs. And she went, and sat her down over against him a good way off, as it were a bowshot: for she said, Let me not see the death of the child. And she sat over against him, and lift up her voice, and wept. And God heard the voice of the lad; and the angel of God called to Hagar out of heaven, and said unto her, What aileth thee, Hagar? fear not; for God hath heard the voice of the lad where he is. Arise, lift up the lad, and hold him in thine hand; for I will make him a great nation. And God opened her eyes, and she saw a well of water; and she went, and filled the bottle with water, and gave the lad drink. And God was with the lad; and he grew, and dwelt in the wilderness, and became an archer. And he dwelt in the wilderness of Paran: and his mother took him a wife out of the land of Egypt (Genesis 21:15-21).

Ishmael wandered in the wilderness with Hagar and ran out of water. After being cast out of his father's house, he found himself dying in the wilderness under a shrub. Hagar could not look upon the pain of her dying son. In hopelessness, she left her son under a bush and walked away, crying out to God. She could not bear seeing her son die. All she could do was weep and cry out in her pain. All the while, the young boy himself lay dying under a bush.

Ishmael went from being a son
to a servant—his identity lay in conflict,
his father image forever shattered.

The young lad was not just physically dying, but his heart was already broken with rejection and his soul pierced with sorrow. In a moment, he went from being a son to merely a servant. "Who am I...the son of a patriarch, the father of many nations, or just the son of a servant?" His identity lay in conflict, and his image of a father was forever shattered. To make matters worse, at the door of death in the wilderness, his own mother left him to die alone. His condition was so bad that his mother could not look at him.

Ishmael was brought up learning about God from his father Abraham; but stranded in the desert, he must have been wondering where his God was. Had God forsaken and forgotten about him? The Bible says that God heard the voice of the lad and knew where he was (see Genesis 21:17). Notice God did not hear the mother but the boy, in the very place he was—the place of death, pain, rejection, and thirst.

God heard the lad because *Ishmael* means "God hears." God knew the end from the beginning; He named Ishmael before he was born because of the plan and destiny for his life. God heard his cry in the wilderness and opened the eyes of Hagar so she could see a well of water and give Ishmael water to drink that he might live. Amazingly, the well was already there, but they could not see it.

The Cry of Ishmael

Four thousand years later, the Muslim people are in a spiritual wilderness, with a cry that has deepened; they are dying of thirst, unable to see the well of their salvation. But God is going to hear the cry of Ishmael and open his eyes and show him the well of living water—Jesus—that he may drink and live. It took water to save his natural life, and it will take living water from the well of Jesus to save his spiritual life.

Water saved Ishmael's natural life;
Living Water will save his spiritual life.

The hour has come for the Muslim people to see Jesus and know the Father. We as a Church must discern the times we are living in and hear the sound of Heaven. We must intercede for the Muslims like a mother would for her dying child. Some of us have walked away from Ishmael, just like his own mother did, because the condition of Ishmael seems so hopeless in many ways; but we must yield to the Spirit of God and pray that God will awaken the cry that is in the hearts of the Muslim people and stir it so deeply that it touches the heart of the Most High.

God will hear the cry of the Muslim people in this hour. God named Ishmael before he was born, in His wisdom, because one day he knew there would be 1.6 billion Muslims in a spiritual wilderness. Church, get ready—an entire generation of Muslims is going to come into the Kingdom. I believe that all of a sudden, 800 million to 1 billion Muslims will enter the Kingdom of God.

An earthquake hit on December 26, 2004, with its epicenter near Indonesia, the largest Muslim nation in the world, causing a tsunami that affected many other nations and caused hundreds of thousands of deaths.

Another earthquake is coming, and the epicenter will be the Muslim people—it will cause a tsunami of the Spirit to go into many other nations, bringing life. This spiritual earthquake will trigger the largest harvest the earth has ever seen.

Intercession and prayer is the first step. Intercession is prayer that embraces the heart of God. The plans of the Spirit are birthed into this realm through prayer. We must not just pray but also be ready to move with God in this hour. God used a woman to give water to Ishmael to drink in the wilderness, and He will use another woman, the Church, to give living water to him today, out of the well of everlasting life. Ishmael is thirsty for living water and hungry for fresh bread baked in the oven of God's Spirit.

Jesus has always been a fisher of humanity. He desires to make us fishers too so we will be ready for this season. To really be fishers of humankind, it is necessary to understand the nature and cry of the Muslim heart.

To understand the nature of the Muslim cry, we must go to the origins of this cry. The cry began when Ishmael was cast out of his father's house and left with no inheritance. For 15 years he grew up with the love of his father, Abraham, but was cast out because the son of the bondwoman could not be heir with the son of the free woman (see Genesis 21:10). Ishmael was cast out into the wilderness with a piece of bread and a bottle of water, the last thing his father ever gave him (see Genesis 21:14).

Ishmael must have looked to his mother for an explanation, but she reminded him that he was the son of a servant and had no father. Ishmael waited in the wilderness, hoping his father would come looking for him and bring him bread and water again; but his father never came. The next time Ishmael saw his father was to bury him (see Genesis 25:9). Ishmael didn't just bury Abraham, he also buried his chance to ever be a son. That burial signified the death of Ishmael's hope to ever be accepted or loved by a father again.

At the core of Ishmael's cry is a desire to be loved by a father and a need for an identity. Without a father, a son has no identity. Identity is not just about who you are but *whose* you are. If you don't know whose you are, you will never know who you are. If you don't know your identity, you define yourself by what you do. A son can be traced by his DNA to his father, but a servant is traced by his works.

Ishmael was cast out and left with no father, identity, or inheritance. With no warning, Ishmael was abandoned, rejected, and fatherless. The right of every son is to receive an inheritance from his father. That right was taken away from Ishmael, leaving him with a seal of his fatherlessness. That cry lives on today in the Muslim people.

The Islam Religion

Centuries later, the children of Ishmael built a memorial around the cry of Ishmael and called it *Islam*, which means to submit to God much like a servant, rather than to have a relationship with him as a son. Islam filled the void of his heart, saying God is not a Father and has no Son. Islam became the face of God to Ishmael. Muslims still see themselves as servants or slaves submitting to God, hoping that, through their works, they can obtain acceptance and approval from God and avoid inevitable judgment. They seek to earn acceptance by God through works rather than grace. This is not just a moral code but the state of being of every Muslim. Regardless, the cry of Ishmael has never ceased but has deepened with time.

> Islam fills the void of a fatherless heart.

Today the Muslim people continue in this wilderness at the point of death. Once again, in this spiritual wilderness, there is a well that they cannot see. They have no father to give them bread or water. At the same time, the Church is walking away from them, unable to watch them die.

God is calling out to the Muslim people in this hour. He will hear their cry and open their eyes and show them the face of Jesus in the well of the living water of the glory of God. God will be their Father and give their hungry souls fresh bread from Heaven and their thirsty hearts living water that they may live. God is going to manifest His glory among Ishmael and revive him in the presence of Jesus.

The Father is going to give an identity to the Muslim people in this hour. He will reveal to them the truth about their destiny hidden in the name of Ishmael. He will show them His covenant and give them an inheritance in Christ Jesus. He will never leave them nor forsake them. Rather, this archer, Ishmael, once born of the Spirit will become an arrow in the bow of God's hand shot right into the heart of the enemy that once blinded him.

God will reveal their destination through the name of Ishmael.

This is the kairos moment for the Muslim people. Bright clouds of God's presence are forming and lightning flashes of His glory are moving over the Muslim world. There will be rain from Heaven and a great harvest of the Muslim people in this hour. The cry of Ishmael has come up before the throne of God, and the answer is on the way.

I can hear God speaking through the prophet Isaiah, saying:

> *I am sought of them that asked not for me; I am found of them that sought me not: I said, Behold me, behold me, unto a nation that was not called by my name* (Isaiah 65:1).

Behold, God is going to do a new thing, and it shall spring forth and make a way in the wilderness and rivers in the desert and we shall all see it (see Isa. 43:19). God will hear the cry of Ishmael in this hour. Will we hear the cry of God's heart in this hour? Will we respond to His cry?

Ministering to a Muslim

I want to share with you about how to minister to a Muslim—how to share your faith with them, how to communicate. I want this to penetrate your heart. In Proverbs 4:23 it says to keep your heart with all diligence for out of it are the issues of life. The picture here is describing a river flowing forth, streams coming forth, life coming forth—out of our heart comes issues and streams that concern life.

In John chapter 7 Jesus is in the midst of celebrating the Feast of Tabernacles and on "the last day, the great day of the feast," He makes a declaration saying, "If you're thirsty, come and drink and I will cause rivers of living water to flow out of your innermost being." (See John 7:37-38.) Notice that He didn't say *river* He said ***rivers***.

If you've been drinking of the Lord Jesus and of that precious living water from Heaven and eating of that fresh bread from Heaven, if you're consuming and digesting that, there's something in you. There's many, many rivers flowing inside of you. One of those rivers is the river of reconciliation, or the ministry of reconciliation, entrusted to every believer. (See 2 Cor. 5:18-19.)

I'm sharing with you something that I have personally lived since I came to Christ. Before God called me into full-time ministry, just individually in my every day life as a businessman, I began to lead people to Christ through various different ways. I saw approximately 1200-1500 people come to know Jesus as their personal savior. I don't have the exact number because I never thought to keep count. But I know at least that many, and probably more, gave their hearts to Christ who were Muslims, Jews, Hindus, Sikhs, and atheists. I'd say that 99 percent of all the people I knew while I was a Muslim are born-again today.

So I'm sharing something with you that I have lived. I'm not just sharing something with you that's written, I'm sharing something with you that is alive *now*. The Bible says we should be *living* epistles read by all people. It's one thing to be a *written* epistle, it's another thing to be a living epistle. (See 2 Cor. 3:2-3.) That has always been the heart of God in the New Covenant—to write His Word and His Laws upon our hearts and put them in our mind so that we can demonstrate and act them out in our lives; so someone can look at your life and say, I've come in contact with a living love letter from Jesus to me.

Before they go to the Book, they should read the Book in you. Before they see Him they should see Him in you and me. Over the years I've realized some things that work and some things that don't. I'm going to share some scriptural principles, and I'm also going to share with you living examples of stories of how I saw people come to Christ.

I know in this particular arena we're going to focus more on the Muslim people, but Second Corinthians chapter 5, verse 17 says:

Therefore if any man be in Christ he's a new creature. Old things have passed away, behold all things are become new. And all things are of God who has reconciled us to Himself by Jesus Christ and has given to us the ministry of reconciliation, to witness that God was in Christ reconciling the world unto himself, not imputing their trespasses unto them and has committed unto us the word of reconciliation. Now then we are ambassadors for Christ as though God did beseech you by us, we pray you in Christ's stead be ye reconciled to God. For He has made Him to be sin for us who knew no sin, that we might be made the righteousness of God in Him.

Notice three things in this Scripture passage. 1) You have been made a new creature. Say, "I'm a new creature." 2) Then it says you have a new ministry. You're a new creature, you have a new ministry. 3) You have a new message or you have a new word of reconciliation. A new message fit for a new creature, a new ministry fit for a new creature. You've become a new creation, something has happened.

That's what happened to me, I became a new creature, and God began to birth something in me, the ministry of reconciliation which is one of those many rivers that flow out of our lives. Now I'll share with you a secret about life—the more you yield to the river that is most prominent within your spirit, the more it will make exit from within your spirit for other rivers in your life. There are rivers of prayer, rivers of your destiny, rivers full of things that the womb of your spirit is pregnant with from Heaven; and when you begin to yield yourself over to the ministry of reconciliation, it will become the doorway to the destiny that God has for your life.

I was called to preach the Gospel before the foundation of the world, I just didn't know it. But I stepped into that arena of my life by yielding to the river of reconciliation. I believe that there is a river of reconciliation inside the heart of every believer, and this river is a river of life. You have life in you to give.

Share the breath of God with others.

You know the *first* Adam was made in such a way that he could breathe the breath of God and live. But the *last* Adam came and gave us life, that we could take the breath of God and that we might be able to give it. The first Adam just barely could live it. We can give it; we can share the breath of God with others. We've been given something to share—rivers of living water, one of those rivers in your life is the ministry of reconciliation. It's already in you; if you yield to the Holy Spirit and cooperate, He'll help you yield to that river inside so you can see results from it.

Sharing and Giving

A Muslim contacted me several years ago. I had just recently become a Christian and there was only one thing I was passionate about and that was, and still is, Jesus being the Son of God. But even before I was in ministry, I knew one thing for sure—Jesus loved people, and He wanted them to be saved. He wanted to know them and wanted them to know Him and His Father. So, this Muslim fellow calls me up and says, "I have 20 questions that no Christian can answer. If you meet with me and you answer these 20 questions, then I will consider your Jesus."

I said, "Yes, I will meet with you," because I knew when it came to salvation, all of Heaven would back me up.

I wasn't quite educated yet; I had come in contact with Christianity and the reality of Jesus, but I wasn't knowledgeable. We met at Perkins, a 24-hour restaurant, on Dixon Road in Toronto. In every booth and every chair of that restaurant someone has come to Christ, someone has been born again.

My pattern: When I would meet with somebody new, I would bring a person along who had just been saved a week or two before. I would train the new believer about how to lead others to the Lord while I was leading a new person to the Lord. I really had no idea what I was doing, but because nobody told me this was unusual in the North American Church, I just kept doing it.

So there I was with this Muslim guy who met with me in the restaurant, and he asked me his first question. While he's asking the question I'm thinking, *I don't even know the answer, it's over. If I can't even answer his first question, what chance do I have of leading this brother to the Lord?* While he finished his question, the answer came to me, and I gave it to him. And I thought, *Wow, I better write that down because that was a good answer!*

Where did that answer come from? To tell you the truth I had no idea, but I knew it came from somewhere, and I knew in my spirit that what I said was true—but I couldn't explain it to you with my mind or prove it to you, but there was a witness who heard it too. I knew it was the truth, and gee it was a good answer; so I shared it with him. And it worked; he asked the second question.

When he asked the next question I did not know the answer again. Again the answer came to me, and I gave it to him. And again I thought I should write it down. This happened each time until he got to the 15th question.

Please notice that I was yielding to the Spirit of God. I was yielding to a river of reconciliation of revelation knowledge that was available at that moment to bring forth wisdom and understanding and truth to this man by the Spirit of God. When he was going to ask me his 15th question, God's tangible presence descended to our booth where we were sitting, and the minute God's presence came into the booth, I looked at the man and said, "That's it, you're finished, it's over!" I said, "God is here, it's finished!"

God is here, it's finished!

That's all I knew as a Muslim—when God comes, it's finished! That's the light I had, that was my revelation. When God came, I was waiting for Him. I didn't know what I was doing anyway, so when He suddenly shows up, I'm thrilled! Thank God it's over.

I turned to the Muslim man and said, "Listen, the Spirit of God is going to grab you from your spirit, He's going to grab you from your belly, and He's going to rise up to your throat." All the while I'm thinking to myself, *what am I saying?* Then the man began to weep uncontrollably; he couldn't compose himself. He couldn't speak, and God's power was upon him. He ran to the bathroom to compose himself. When he came back to the booth and tried to speak, he began weeping again and ran to the bathroom again to compose himself. I like that kind of ministry.

Now the man's questions began to change—they were no longer coming from his mind, they were coming from his spirit. They were humble; they were genuine. They were sincere. And I love those kinds of questions. Then I began to answer his questions, and the 20th question was: how do I know what you're telling me is the truth?

I turned to him and said, "Because your spirit is drawn and attracted to the truth, and truth is a person. His name is Jesus, and He lives on the inside of me, and your spirit wants Him too." Then I said to myself, *that's a good answer!*

His 21st question: "How do I make this Jesus my Lord?" I took him to my "save-mobile" car, along with the gentleman who was with me, and we began to lead him into the prayer of salvation. God's presence was in the car, and he gave his heart to Christ—there is nothing better than that. One-on-one experiencing the life of God entering into a human heart and seeing the fruit of that life begin to germinate—that's the best.

After he received Christ, he was healed of asthma too, but we had no idea at the time. He went home that evening, and called me the next morning. He said, "You know, all my life as a Muslim I had never been able to sleep at night. For the first time in my life I actually slept last night." He said, "Usually my mind is awake all night, I'm thinking, my body might be sleeping in and out, but I never sleep. It was for the first time I actually slept. I had this unusual peace, what is this?"

I said, "This is Jesus."

Meditation Moment

Based on the Scriptures and my experiences you read about, honestly reflect upon the relationship Ishmael had with his father, Abraham, and his mother. Then put yourself in his place. Can you get past the hurt, anger, and resentfulness? Now think about the multimillions of Muslims who have lived with generations of these feelings. How can we not share the love of Jesus with them.

Endnote

1. http://www.islamicpopulation.com/.

Chapter 2

The River of Reconciliation

Yielding

WHAT happened to change the man with the 20 questions? I yielded to the river of reconciliation, the ministry entrusted to every believer; and because I didn't know enough with my head, I had to depend on the Spirit. Then the spirit of revelation began to operate and come forth, and those things in the river that are inside began to minister life. We are never intended to minister life any other way but by the Spirit that is on the inside of you. That's why you're the temple of God. We're a walking, talking, breathing temple of the Spirit of God. There are no limitations to where you can go.

Because of yielding to the river of reconciliation, everywhere we minister today is because of someone I led to the Lord years ago. By yielding to the river in my life, doors have been opened by people who went on to become pastors or members of various Churches. And lo and behold God began to move me into the destiny of what I was called for—He opened doors for a television program, because my wife, Sabina, and I are called to media ministry. The ministry we have today began because I was leading people to the Lord, because I was yielding to the river of reconciliation that opened the door to my destiny.

I was called to the ministry of reconciliation. In your case, you might be a businessperson. As an example, I heard the story of a man who is born-again, and he worked for the National Aeronautics and Space Administration (NASA). He is the gentleman responsible for designing the wings on satellites that orbit the earth today. In the early days of space exploration, NASA launched satellites in hopes of obtaining information. These satellites cost an enormous amount of money, and unfortunately many would disappear into space. They had no way to control the satellites' movements.

Yield to the river's flow.

One time this man showed up at a prayer meeting and a word of the Lord came forth through tongues and interpretation and the Lord spoke to the man, "wings like birds, wings like birds." He began to design wings that control the satellites. He's not a preacher, but he was fulfilling his destiny—to makes wings for satellites so the Gospel could be spread worldwide through satellite signals to televisions and radios. He yielded to a river in his life.

Many of you have cries, many of you have great things in your spirit, and I tell you this: When you yield to the river of reconciliation it will open the door to destiny in your life. There's not one thing that Sabina and I do today that is not connected to that river in my life. Whatever that river is in your life, the more you yield to it the better.

Why do I mention the concept of this river of revelation flowing from your spirit? Because Muslim people respond to revelation. They do not respond to mental gymnastics and debates, they do not respond to arguments. Muslim's love to debate, but when you debate, an argument may convince someone's mind, but their mind is subject to change. I'm not after people's *minds*; I want to be a fisher of people's *hearts*. Jesus said, "I will make you fishers of men,"—not men who are great at arguing with the faculties of their mind. (See Mark 1:17.)

While I was in Pakistan one year, I saw some very interesting things. I witnessed the rituals that Muslims perform to be healed on the eve of the festival of sacrifice honoring Abraham's sacrifice. They believe that Abraham took Ishmael, not Isaac, to the altar to be sacrificed. In fact they believe he was going to be sacrificed on the mount on which the Dome of the Rock is situated; but instead, a ram was caught in the thickets and used as the sacrifice.

That's what Muslims do, in order to honor that event every year, they have animal sacrifices throughout the Muslim nations and Islamic Republics, including Pakistan. The particular ritual consists of dipping a ring in goat's blood for three days and praying Qur'anic verses over it. As long as a person wears the ring, that person will remain disease free. But as a result, the person makes a covenant with an entity that dominates their soul. They trade their soul for something else.

As I was on the plane back to Canada, I began to talk to the Lord about what I saw in Pakistan. I asked, "Lord, what is your answer?" When I considered that nation with so many people, I said, "Lord, how are these people going to know who Jesus is?" He said, "For five years bombard this nation with media and the nation will change."

But then He also began to show me something about the Muslim world. I said how, "How is this going to happen?" He told me that the day is going to come when they are going to call on the door of the Church, these Muslim people, particularly in our generation, and they're going to ask you to debate them. God said, "When they ask you to debate them I want you to say no."

But He also said, "When you're prepared and ready, and when there are people prepared in the Church and they're ready, then I'm going to release people." And He said, "I want you to say, 'I won't have a debate with you, but we'll have a demonstration. Bring the dead, bring them with no limbs, bring them with no arms, bring those who are dying,' and say to them, 'Now come and demonstrate who is the God of all power!' And in the name of Jesus demonstrate My power! And say 'We're not going to have an argument; we're going to have a demonstration of the power of God!'" That is an era that is coming to the North American Church.

"In the name of Jesus
demonstrate My power!"

Then I saw universities and auditoriums filled with people saying, "We're going to find out whose God is really God! And we're going to find out who Jesus really is." He said, "We will settle it with power, because arguments do not settle it." That's why I don't debate with Muslims. We're living in an era of power and demonstration of the Spirit, and that's going to take yielding to the river that is in us. Just like there's a river of reconciliation, there are other rivers inside of you.

Compassion

There is another key strategy I'd like to share with you about sharing the Gospel. The following is an example of yielding to the river of reconciliation. I went to a hospital to visit a friend, because he had been sick and was having some kind of minor operation. When I was in the hospital hallway, I noticed all of the beds; and a white-haired, older gentleman who was speaking on the phone and very distraught caught my attention. The minute I looked at his face, a wave of compassion came over me. As it did, I felt compelled to walk over to him.

While he was still on the phone I interrupted him and said, "Sir, what do you want?" He looked up at me while holding the phone, and I asked him again, "Sir, what do you want?"

He put the phone down and said, "My wife. She was here three months ago and was diagnosed with cancer and the doctor said she'd be dead in three months. It's been three months and my wife is lying over there on the bed. She is unconscious and the doctors have refused to look at her because they say there is nothing more they can do."

I said, "Sir, what do you want?"

I had never done such a thing before—walk up to someone in a hospital and ask them what they wanted. But I said again, "What do you want?"

This time he said, "I want my wife to live."

"How long do you want her to live? I asked him.

He said, "Three months."

"Can you take a year?"

He looked at me puzzled. I asked again, "Can you take a year?"

He said, "Yes!"

"Can you take three years?"

He said, "Yes!"

The gift of faith came upon me, and I knew by the Spirit of God that up to three years was guaranteed. Do you know what I'm talking about? It wasn't *my* faith. It was the *gift of faith* that fell on me, and I knew at that moment that I could pray for his wife.

"If I can pray for your wife, I believe that Jesus is going to heal her and give her back to you."

"Please come," the man said. So I prayed for his wife and the minute I laid hands on her and rebuked the cancer, the power of God went into her. Her complexion changed, and she opened her eyes. There was an immediate change in her, and the husband was shocked, he quickly turned to me and said, "Oh thank you, thank you!"

"No, no, don't thank me, let me tell you about Jesus!" I knew this was an opportunity for salvation, so I shared the Gospel with him. He looked at me, and I asked him, "Do you want to receive Jesus into your life?"

He said yes, and he prayed with me. With tears in his eyes he turned to me and said, "This morning when I got up to bring my wife to the hospital, I looked out the window and I saw a man clothed in white with a bright shining face, and he was smiling—now I know that was Jesus!"

The man got saved because I cooperated with something in the Spirit that was already organized, and I just happened to be there. I could not have orchestrated that with my mind. I yielded to the river of love inside of me. Compassion is not how someone feels about their situation, it's not even how you feel about them. That's pity, not compassion!

Compassion is the heart of God for that person and at that moment you get a live download of the overwhelming compassion of God for that person. And every time compassion comes, it opens the doorway to the gifts of the Spirit in operation. Compassion will open the gifts of the Spirit.

Compassion, not pity.

First Corinthians 14:1 says, "Pursue love and desire spiritual gifts...." Yes you desire spiritual gifts, yes you covet earnestly the best gifts, but the priority is to pursue love. When you pursue love, it opens the door to the river and the life of God. The gifts of the Spirit were in operation when I didn't even know what they were. I hadn't been educated yet.

In fact, after I got educated, they started to decrease. I'm being honest with you. I'm not opposing education, but what we need is training. Education will inform you and tickle your mind, but *training* will equip you and impart something in you to move you into action. I was being trained, and I didn't even know it. In the process, because I pursued the love of Jesus for that person or for the people around me, and I yielded to the love that was shed abroad in my heart by the Holy Spirit, it opened the door to whatever was needed at the time to get the job done.

There's no real way to mess up when you're sharing Jesus with someone. There *is* no formula. There is a formula, though, if you want to get someone "brain saved." I've seen a lot of brain-saved people in the Church. Half of my ministry is getting brain-saved people saved! Have you met brain-saved people? Just sitting in Church doesn't make you a Christian, likewise just sitting in the garage doesn't make you a car.

Your heart must open, your spirit has to be regenerated. When I talk to Muslim people, I say, "Hold on a minute let's forget about your mind, let's talk about your spirit."

Their response is, "What? You mean my soul?"

"No, no, no, let's talk about your *spirit*. You have a spirit man, I want to talk to him for a moment."

"Spirit? Really?" they say.

"Yes, let's talk about what's in your heart." That opens the door; because when you love their heart, God will come and back you up. You must realize that attitude to be successful in the ministry of reconciliation. I'm speaking from experience. As a Muslim, to me the Word of God is valuable because since childhood I was taught how important the Qur'an was—and was willing to die for a book. Now I can live for not just a book, but the Living Word about whom the Book testifies and reveals.

Jesus said when you search the Scriptures, they testify and they reveal Him. At the end of the day *who* is being revealed to you makes all the difference. So when you become a living epistle read of all people, everywhere you go they will see that river flowing from you—spilling out of you and giving life.

Another strategy key—wait for people to ask you questions. With the exception of supernatural things like what happened in the hospital, every person I've led to the Lord, even every Muslim, this rule applies to. I do not jump and thump! I wait for them to ask me questions. When compassion overwhelms me, I yield to the Holy Spirit in anyway possible. But I look for the wisdom of God because the Book of Proverbs says that "he who winneth souls is wise." (See Proverbs 11:30.) It doesn't mean you get wise by winning souls, it means you have to be wise in order to win souls. Apostle Paul also writes of this to the Church in Corinth, "that the world by their wisdom knew not God" (1 Cor. 1:21).

The fruit of wisdom.

The true test of wisdom—do you know God and can you reveal God? That's the fruit of wisdom. What is wisdom? It is revelation concealed. What is revelation? It is wisdom revealed.

Questions and Answers

There are mysteries concerning people's lives that are hidden in God. When you yield yourself to the Spirit and when you yield yourself to love, God will give you the right thing to say at the right time to minister to people. You need to be looking for answers to their questions in their heart.

Most of my life I have desired to answer people's questions. They ask me questions, and I look for ways to find answers to their questions by yielding to the Spirit of God and to the wisdom of the Scriptures. In seeking answers I find that their hearts open up. Questions are the keys to unlocking the human heart. Not just questions they know about, but also the "silent questions."

There are silent questions in the human heart, especially every Muslim heart. There are deep, suppressed questions, and if you learn to answer those silent questions by the Spirit of God, you will bring others to the saving knowledge of Jesus Christ. Through my experiences, I'm hoping to train your spirit to learn how to grasp and capture answers from the Spirit. Yielding to Him will allow those answers to come out through your life, through your DNA, through your personality.

You can't copy me; you can't copy anybody. If you try to copy somebody else, at best you're going to be a second-class somebody else. I would rather encourage you to be a first-class you! Be a first-class, unique expression of Jesus in the way you are, and express Jesus the way you do. And you'll see people come to Christ your way. I'm just sharing from my life experiences and hoping that you will learn things that will help you lead others to the Lord—but in your own way. The principle is the same: it's the same Spirit. But there's many ways that He begins to operate and express Himself. Remember: the river is inside of you and that is the river of reconciliation that needs to come forth.

Muslim people have a servant mentality. Because of Ishmael they still believe in salvation by works. Their mind-set is to serve—they do not understand grace. What is grace? Many times *grace* is defined as "unmerited favor." What does that mean? Grace is the divine influence of God to the human heart to cause a response to the heart of people without violating their free will. That's the grace of God.

We have to yield to the Spirit of God, yield to that grace, and allow the Holy Spirit to control us. Have you noticed a time when God influenced and touched your heart in spite of being hardened or stubborn in your mind? You may have realized that there was a change in your heart, and you responded to God? We are all products of grace. The grace of God went into your heart. Now where does this grace abide? It abides in our spirit. Is that true? If so, we have to let it bubble up from within us, and it needs to influence the rest of our lives and our whole beings—it must be tangible for people to see it.

Talk to the heart rather than argue with the mind.

God's grace needs to come out from us and touch other people's lives. That's the grace of God, it needs to come forward. Learn to talk to the heart of a person rather than argue with the mind of a person. The arguments of a man's mind are mere walls and examples of fear that guard the very nature and heart of what they carry. All arguments are fear mechanisms and walls put up like a castle to guard their hearts. But if you can penetrate by the Spirit beyond the wall, then you'll become a first-time visitor into the real "home" or heart of a person. When you get there, they will know it. I've discovered that no one comes to the Son except when the Father draws him.

Do you remember that statement I made to the Muslim man in the restaurant? I told him that his spirit is drawn and attracted to the truth. There's a drawing that takes place—you don't draw people, the Father draws them. How does He do it? By the Spirit of God; He draws them by His Son. So I wait for the signs of drawing. In my experience, their questions usually change over time. If you've led anybody to the Lord, you've probably noticed that their questions begin to change.

They become very sincere, and their questions eventually come from their heart. You'll know it, don't worry, you'll know because you'll be aware of God. You'll be conscious of His love; you'll be conscious of Him. God's going to help you, and when you begin to yield to a place you know not of, when you begin to step out of the faculty of everything programmed and organized in your mind, you'll begin to taste the true meaning of the Christian life. You'll experience the river, and it is exciting! When the river of God flows and people come to Christ, you'll rejoice. After the Muslim was saved at Perkins's, I went home, and I rejoiced. I jumped! I was more excited than he was because I discovered something that was in my spirit, and it was a river—flowing from God's grace.

Sometimes your life can clog up your river, sometimes your education can clog the life of God in you. Let's be honest. The river is the first thing we want to tap into. I'd like to be a drill and drill deep into the well of your spirit—I want to tap into the life that is already residing in you.

Many times we say things like, God we want rain to come, revival to come, we want God to fall, we want power to come; we're saying, "Rain down from Heaven." But a lot of times we forget about the wells that must be dug in our own lives before these things can happen. We need to unclog the deep wells of deposits that God has made in our lives. The minute that you drill into the core of your spirit and release the river's flow, you will become a living epistle read of all men. You'll become a unique, genuine, expression of Christ. You will no longer be a copy, you will no longer be a formula, you'll no longer say "here are the four rules, and this is what you need to do next." When people come in contact with you, they will come in contact with the Greater One inside you.

Another time a Muslim man came to me. I'm sharing these stories from my life experiences to encourage you first...before I give you mechanics. If I give you only mechanics you will have a formula, but you won't carry the spirit of it—you'll be a mechanic rather than a living epistle.

So I met this Muslim fellow one afternoon. He told me that he used to see me at the Perkins's Restaurant on Sunday nights when I'd gather all the people who were saved, and I tried to answer their questions. A Muslim man, who had recently been saved, and I talked with him about Jesus. The man listened to what we had to say, then he went home. He came back later and said, "I want to talk to you."

"OK, what is it?"

"I want to know how I can know this Jesus," he said.

At the time I was a little young at this so I always made sure everyone was "qualified" to pray. I asked him, "Are you sure you want Jesus? Are you willing to give your whole life to Him, everything? Do you really want Jesus?" Now I'll take them the way they come, but back then they had to qualify. So I'd interview everybody before I prayed with them to make sure it was real. There is some power in that, by the way. That's why people we've seen come to Christ over the years still walk with Christ, because their experience with Christ was genuine.

So I asked this Muslim man, "So why do you want to come to Jesus now, what changed?"

He said, "Well, for two years every time I'm near you this Presence comes on me."

I didn't know that! Do you see how this works? What was I doing? Pursuing love, I had no idea this man was being affected by what I was doing in the restaurant.

He said, "For two years this has happened to me, but when I go home I brush it off. It goes away. Today this Presence came on me, it followed me home, and it hasn't left me. And I know that I have to know this Jesus!"

Now how hard was that? What mental, intellectual debate did I have with this Muslim?

I said, "OK, you're qualified, we need to pray with you." And we prayed with this brother, and he was born again. I attended his wedding not long afterward, it was such a blessing to see him get married. He gave his heart to Christ because His presence became real.

If Christianity is just like every other religion, then why are Christians different to others who see the grace of God flowing from you? Every religion has light, knowledge, some kind of illumination. But if all you have is light, what sets you apart? True light is an actual expression of the life of God. That's why in John 1:4, John speaking of Jesus says, "in Him was life and the life was a light unto men." The light we have is an expression of His life—tangible substance from Him. If all you have is knowledge you'll get puffed up. But if you have love you'll get built up, and you'll be able to share that with others.

Love builds you up to share with others.

I'm quietly and gently and lovingly...hopefully kindly, trying to help you make a little adjustment—to switch over to expressing love first. I shared with you how the heart of God imparted something to your spirit of faith, and an encouragement. This is how God sees Muslims. If you don't see them the way Jesus sees them you're not going to be able to love them the way Jesus loves them.

And when that love comes forth, it brings forth all that God is, and most of the time Muslims get saved this way in our ministry—because we love them. I love them, without a motive. I love them whether they ever come to Christ or not. I love them because I love them! Remember I'm not the one who can make it happen—only the Holy Spirit can. But in loving all people, His presence comes, and His gifts go into operation.

Dreams and Visions

Another strategy to win Muslims to the Lord is dreams and visions. When God said to me that a whole generation of Muslims is about to come into the Kingdom, I asked Him a question, "God, how shall this be?" And He told me there were five things that would happen. (All five are explained in the next chapter.)

One of the things He shared with me is, "I am going to do it with dreams and visions. I am going to visit the Muslim people in dreams and visions and re-awaken the cry of their hearts so that they will seek Me out for the answers." God will respond to the cry of Ishmael with dreams and visions of Jesus. The answer to these dreams and visions will be the Gospel of Christ, which is the power of God unto salvation. Imagine millions of Muslims looking for answers to their visions about Jesus, the man clothed in white with holes in his hands saying "*I am the way, the truth, and the life*" (John 14:6).

These dreams and visions will grip their consciousness, and their hearts will forever long to search out the Father who is drawing them. In search of truth they will knock on the door of the mosque; they will look everywhere. They are going to come to the Church looking for answers. The Church must be ready to tell them who Jesus is. I know from experience that Muslims pay extra attention to their dreams, because they believe God can speak to them through their dreams. Muslims believe God has not spoken audibly since the death of Mohammad, the prophet of Islam, thus leaving dreams as avenues of communication to their hearts.

Love will interpret
a heart's dream.

The open door in their understanding is dreams and visions. As a Muslim, I paid careful attention to my dreams and there are even certain specific times during the year in the Muslim calendar when Muslims pray and believe that they will have a vision. Some believe that if they have a vision, they can get a free ticket to Heaven. But most of the time they have to work on earning "air miles" to get them high enough to enter Heaven. So dreams and visions are a major key in the Islamic religion.

If we're not yielding to love, we're not yielding to the river of reconciliation; and we're not going to open the door for the Holy Spirit to help us to interpret dreams. If you don't love their heart you can't interpret the dream of their heart.

That's another thing I do when I'm with a Muslim. I try to identify their spirit, try to identify and locate where their heart is. And I begin to talk with their heart rather than argue with their head. And if I don't get anywhere I say something like, "Hey listen, have you had any dreams lately?" Lo and behold, most of the time, they share two or three dreams with me. One of them is genuinely from God.

If you love the person you won't even have to ask, the Holy Spirit will give you the interpretation and when you interpret the dream...now you've got their attention. They will ask you how you knew the interpretation. They will be drawn to the truth, and you will know that God is with you. And they will be drawn to Him.

When the heart opens and the eyes open wide, the guard comes down. Now you know it's time. Ask them, are you ready? Most time I wait for them to ask me. Dreams and visions are keys to Muslim people's reality. We as the Church must yield ourselves to God, and He'll help us. I'm giving you practical keys to reach them.

It's about yielding to the Spirit. That's pretty simple isn't it? But you see the Gospel is simple. It's the simplicity of Christ. Yielding allows the Holy Spirit to give the interpretation which attracts their attention—but it all starts with loving them!

Remember the Muslim man who got saved after asking me 20 questions? For six months afterward he hung out with me and another believer. We asked him why.

"Well the truth is, for six months I felt an unconditional love from you folks that I never felt before, and I couldn't understand it. But I was drawn to this thing in you guys. At the same time I was pulled, and I was provoked and I was hardened to stick in my belief, and that's why I wanted to challenge everything. All along my heart was being drawn to it."

You see, don't be moved by the hard shell of a person. I was cold-hearted; I was stone-hearted. God would rather we be cold or hot than lukewarm because when you decide where you stand He'll say, "Now that you've made your decision, I can deal with you." (See Revelation 3:16.)

I made a decision to be cold, and I was one of the "frozen chosen." But something changed in me when I accepted Jesus—I became a new creature. I was just a Muslim, but because of the Holy Spirit and the Lord, and because of the truth in His Word, I yielded to the river of reconciliation. I didn't even know what I was doing, but I knew I had to share my joy with other Muslims. I was not really doing anything, I was just yielding to Someone who knows the end at the beginning.

I find many times that we've trained people so well that they are good on the theory, but they don't know how to actually bring others to Christ. When people first come to Christ there is a zeal. There needs to be a balance between zeal and knowledge.

How do you use dreams and visions to share the love of Christ? First you get into the Scriptures—meditate on them, come before the Lord and digest the Scriptures. Let the Holy Spirit touch your heart, and let the love be birthed in you. When you let the love flow, you will say the right thing at the right time to the right person—yield to it!

If you feel like you need to ask, "Did you have a dream lately?" and they begin to tell you, the Holy Spirit will begin to interpret. You simply say, "Would you like to know what that dream means?"

The reply will most probably be, "Yes, I would really like to know!" That's what Muslims say to me.

If you don't know what to say, just tell them that you're going to pray about it. Say, "I'm going to ask Jesus. I'm going to ask my Father, and I'm going to come back to you. We're going to talk about this dream again. Is that all right?"

You don't have to interpret the dream on the spot. Go home, get before the Lord, and ask Him to fill you with so much love that the interpretation will come with it. Many times we try to figure everything out. It's not figuring everything out; it's living it out. In the process of living it; understanding will come. That's why the Bible says to *hear* the Word and *do* the Word. (See James 1:22.) Because when you hear the Word and you begin to do the Word, more and more understanding comes in the process.

Don't figure it out, live it out.

Light and Life

We have life that becomes light. What is *life*? It is revelation written on our hearts. What is *light*? It's the illumination of that revelation in our hearts coming up in our minds. Understanding comes when we see truth and we walk in that truth. Become a doer of the Word to build your life for Him.

That type of life attracts Muslims; because they're not looking for a moment with you, they're looking at your life. When they see that your life is different, you have their attention. Most of the Muslims who came to the Lord before I was in the ministry didn't receive Christ right away. For some it took months for others it took years, but they all did because I just kept loving them.

When they had questions they knew they could come to me because I would genuinely try to give them answers based on the Scriptures and the Holy Spirit's leading.

When I'd get to an answer of their heart's cry they'd say, "Wait a minute...how did you know the answer to my heart?"

I told them, "It's not me, it's my God who revealed that answer through my relationship and walking with Him. You can have that relationship too." That's why they give themselves over to Christ.

Many Muslims will want to debate with you over certain scriptures. I will give you some insight into that, but now I want you to understand the heart of the matter. If you only have a response formula, then you are really no different than they are. But if you become a living epistle...then they will see Jesus flowing out of you—something that will attract their attention.

John 3:8 says you can hear the wind blowing and coming from one direction and going in the next direction. You can't tell from where it comes, you can't tell where it goes. So are they that are born of the Spirit. If you're born of the Spirit you can't be labeled or figured out.

As Muslims notice that you are a living epistle, they can't quite figure you out and they wonder what is different about you. When they ask, you can tell them you're different because of Jesus—it's the wind of the Spirit, it's the light I've been born of, it's the source of which I come from, it's the life that is written in my heart, it's the living epistle He's called me to be.

Truth and Terror

There is a shaking coming in the Muslim world. It's not by accident, be not concerned, for it is the undercurrent that is below the Muslim nations. It is the undercurrent of the Spirit of God that is flowing in the Muslim nations. It is a heavy undercurrent that is brewing beneath the Muslim hearts and is causing things to come to the surface. So be not concerned, for there will be wars and rumors of wars but be not concerned—it is not the end but merely the beginning.

But look at the heart and look at what God is saying, for the Spirit of God is doing a mighty work. He's preparing the hearts of the nations; He's preparing the hearts of people groups. God says that we should not be concerned about new mosques that are being raised up, and new mosques that are being built around the world—even some that are the largest in the world. But be it known that those buildings one day will be changed into sanctuaries of My glory, and My presence will descend and many Muslims will see Jesus and they'll be saved. God says that they are building Me a dwelling place because I will come and change the name on the wall to the name of My Son.

The power of God is going to flow—be not afraid nor terrified for there are even more shakings coming. Be it known that you rest in the life of God and in His truth that is made known to you in His Word. Yield to the Spirit and drink of the life that is resident in you, for there is a river of living water inside you. This river is not just for your drinking but for others too. This is a river of life that flows in you, for them who are lost and dying and thirsty in the wilderness, for they need a drink too. Yield to that.

Just like the terrorists, there's a radical breed in the Church, but they won't be radical in the natural, they'll be radical in the spirit. They will be bold. You're going to see the fear and the boldness of God come upon men and women in this era because He's raising up people; and while they are yet speaking, the Spirit of

God will fall on them who hear the Word, and they'll be filled with the Spirit in the midst of their terror.

There's a boldness coming to the Church. For even terror will look into the eyes of the Church and see the fire and the flame in the eyes of Jesus and terror will bow. It's not going to bow right away though. There will be a demise, but before the demise there will be things that will increase. They will increase because when you cast a devil or a demon out of someone, on the way out it makes a bit of a fuss! A devil doesn't know when to stop when he's losing control. God's light exposes the enemy so he loses control, and on his way down he causes trouble.

But the day is coming when you will see Muslim terrorists blow up their own Muslim people, and they will not be able to separate between Christians and Jews. Then they will realize that something is wrong because the devil will be totally, fully exposed. About that time you will see the demise.

The wall of Islam has fallen.

The Lord spoke to me; He said the wall of Islam has fallen in the spirit that has kept the Muslim people hostage. He said, "It is only a matter of time when it becomes common knowledge that the wall of Islam has fallen! Because I've heard the cry of the Muslim people from behind the wall and it's come up to the throne, I will respond because I've been moved because I've put a cry in them, and I will hear the cry of Ishmael. For what the Church has considered a mistake, for what the Church has written off, for what the Church has considered foolishness, I will use in these last days and I will bring him forth, for I have a purpose for him."

So we, the Church, need to get serious—our hearts have to be hearts of love.

Saul was a terrorist of the early Church; he didn't have bombs, but he had stones. He was involved in killing people. He was wreaking havoc in the Church. God visited that terrorist, and he bit the dust before the majesty of Jesus.

His Glory

The Muslim world is about to have a head-on collision with the glory of God! And the glory of God is going to bring about a change that no man can alter. For light eliminates darkness, but the glory of God dispels gross darkness! Be it known that the glory of the Lord shall stand up and deal with gross darkness in the land. Arise and shine for the light has come, the glory of the Lord has risen upon us. There may be darkness in the world and gross darkness on the people. But His glory shall arise on you, and He shall be seen in you.

Prepare for a
head-on collision with God.

We're moving into an era of the glory of the Lord coming and the weightiness of His glory shall descend into the earth. There's a greater measure of His glory that is being released in this era. There's an open door in the Spirit. It is a door of Heaven that is opening for transportation of the weightiness of God to come down. For there are a people who have been setting themselves apart, there are a people who have been before His throne. He's saying that if you will become a container collectively through love, then you can inhabit more of Him.

His glory is coming. I've seen the glory happen to Muslims. The glory of God came upon them, and they were changed. When I had a head-on collision with the glory of God, something changed for me. No argument can stand in the courts of Heaven because when you get into that realm, the counsel of Heaven will cut out the question of your heart and the argument that you have in your mind.

Do you know that Muslims want to kill me? Why am I still preaching and writing? Because if I don't depend on Him and I don't trust in Him, what hope do I have anywhere? If I don't have Him—I'm finished!

Strategically and slowly the North American Church has allowed some things to settle in that are clogging the well. I believe that something is going to happen in the Spirit in cities where the backbone of Islam is going to be broken. It takes time for things to manifest in the natural. Don't look at them as your enemy; Ananias saw Saul, Jesus appeared to him in a vision and told him to go pray for Saul in the city.

Ananias said, "Excuse me, Jesus, do you know who this guy is? This guy is a terrorist; he's messed up. He's caused so much trouble."

Jesus said, "Listen, he is a chosen vessel unto me. I will show him what he must suffer for my namesake, and he'll bear My name before kings and gentiles in all of Israel." (See Acts 9)

This is the same word I want to say to you. Ishmael is a chosen vessel unto God in these times. He's going to bear His name in a powerful way in the earth. He's got to suffer much, but Ishmael was an archer and God walked with him in the Book of Genesis chapter 21. God is going to get this archer born of the Spirit and once he is born of God, he will become an arrow in the bow of God's hand—He will fire him into the heart of the enemy. And what the enemy has held hostage will be set free.

I hear a shaking in the prison walls that are going collapse. I see bars that have gone so deep in the foundation of the ground that they look like they're impossible to move! But there's going to be a Holy Ghost earthquake in the Spirit realm that will open the prison bars that have held many peoples hostage with gross darkness!

We need His glory to deal with them, and love is the way to the glory. Love is the doorway to the glory, love is the legs that carries the glory. God is love, but He is the Father of glory. Glory precedes forth from Him, but He is love. When you become an expression of love, glory will precede forth also. Isaiah 60 says that the glory shall be seen *on* you.

I believe the glory of God will descend upon the nations, but it won't be all fun and games when it happens. There's a whole lot more to it. But prepare yourselves a sanctuary by the Spirit of God to be a dwelling place, not just a visiting place of the manifestation of the Spirit of God.

Meditation Moment

Flowing in the river of reconciliation means allowing your traditions, prejudices, culture, selfishness, and pride to be swept far away while you continue moving along with God's current within the confines of His merciful riverbanks. Refresh yourself with His living water—then splash it over those around you.

Chapter 3

Muslims Through God's Eyes

GOD uses the foolish things of this world to confound the wise (see 1 Cor. 1:27). Just when we think we know everything, God comes along and uses that which we think is not useful. It is amazing how the one we judge or give up on is the very same person God will reach out to. I was one of those people.

Prior to Sunday, July 3, 1994, at 12:45 P.M., I was a Muslim adamantly opposed to the Gospel of the Lord Jesus Christ. Born in Pakistan as a Sunni Muslim, I was brought up subconsciously to oppose the deity of Jesus. For years, after school every day, I would go straight to a special school to study the Qur'an—a required part of a Muslim youngster's life.

I was taught and believed Jesus to be no more than a prophet, second to Muhammad. Like all Muslims, I believed that confessing or believing that Jesus was the Son of God was the worst unforgivable sin a Muslim could ever commit. I considered such confession to be blasphemy. I believed the Bible was changed and inaccurate.

Later in life as a Canadian businessman, I debated with many Christians, attempting to convert them to Islam. When invited to Church, my response would be, "I don't go to Church; I am a Muslim." One night while attending a business convention in the United States with approximately 20,000 people, I was invited to a non-denominational Christian service on Sunday morning. I was promised a front-row seat that I could use after the service for the remainder of the business convention.

I took the bait and showed up the next morning. I noticed that the first 30-40 rows of seats were missing on the main floor in front of the stage. Puzzled, I asked a lady about the empty space in front of the stage. Her response, "Something is going to happen here today." As I inquired further, she said, "Don't worry. You will soon find out." My curiosity got the best of me, and I found a seat as close to the front as possible.

A businessman got up to speak, and he declared that Jesus is the Son of God. I could not believe what he was saying, and I became angry. He went on to say that there was no name given among men by whom one could be saved except the name of Jesus, and if any one rejected Him as Lord and did not believe on the Son of God, that person would go to hell. I did not like that.

Then he had the audacity to say, "There are only two books which claim to be the written Word of God—the Bible is, and the other one is not." I knew he was talking about my book. I thought this man was deceived and decided to talk to him and straighten him out. Then he gave an altar call. I wasn't sure what an altar was, or a call, but I was one of the first to run to the front, thinking this would be my chance to speak to this man.

From all directions, thousands rushed to the front to receive Jesus as their Savior. I thought about leaving, but I couldn't because I was stuck to the stage because of all the people around me. Then the man proceeded to lead us in a prayer that began with "Jesus is the Son of God." I said, "No way," and confessed my *Kalma* as a Muslim instead.

On my way back to my seat, two friends tried to hug and congratulate me for going to the front to give my heart to Jesus. I asked if they were crazy and declared, "I am a Muslim; don't ever call me a Christian. The earth could shake and the mountains could move, but there is nothing on this earth that could ever make me confess that your Jesus is the Son of God."

"...nothing...could make me confess Jesus as the Son of God."

In a few months, I went to another convention and went to the Sunday service to save a seat and heard a businessman get up to preach Jesus as Lord. An altar call was given, and a second time I ran to the front; thousands followed. Immediately, I realized those people were being evangelized into Christianity through the preaching of the Gospel. I made a determined decision while at the altar that I would learn what the people do, and I would do it better than they do it and would convert Christians in particular to Islam. After making that decision, I proceeded with my plans.

A few months later, I went to a third business convention in the United States. I now understood Christian terminology and understood that when someone said they were "born again," it meant that they had received Jesus as their personal Lord and Savior and became a child of God. I got myself a front seat. Someone got up and preached that one can become a child of God and know God as Father through Jesus Christ, His only begotten Son. He went on to say that Jesus is the only way, the truth, and the life. After his preaching, he asked us all to stand, so we all stood. Then he began to give an altar call. This time I did not go to the front.

God's presence permeated through me.

As I was standing there, suddenly the living God showed up. At once, God's presence permeated through me, encircled and arrested me. Engulfed in His Holy presence, immediately I knew I stood before God. My entire existence faded; He was all that mattered. When God shows up, you will know it with every fiber of your being—spirit, soul, and body. I had many questions going through my mind, but the longer I stood before Him, my questions disappeared.

I asked Him one sincere question, "God, what are You doing here? I thought these were the bad guys [referring to the Christians]?" I could not understand why God would manifest Himself among a people who were blaspheming God by worshiping Jesus as the Son of God. The answer came, and I heard these words, "*No, these are my children.*" Again, "*No, these are my children,"* and a third time, *"No, these are my children."* His words echoed right through me, and immediately the veil was removed from my eyes.

I knew nothing else but this reality that *Jesus is the Son of God!* This same Jesus whom I fervently denied, I now could not live without. I went forward and confessed with my own mouth that Jesus is the Son of God, He was born of a virgin, died on the Cross, and shed His blood for me; and I believed in my heart that God raised Him from the dead on the third day. My prayer was, "Father, take away my stony heart and give me a new heart of flesh. Jesus, come into my heart, be my Lord, that I may love the Father even as Thee." I became a new creation on that Sunday, July 3, 1994, at 12:45 P.M.

I know by revelation that Jesus is the Son of God. In Matthew 16:15-17, Jesus turned and asked His disciples, *"But whom say ye that I am?"* Peter answered and said, *"Thou art the Christ, the Son of the living God."* Jesus responded and said to him, *"Flesh and blood hath not revealed it unto thee, but My Father which is in heaven."* Peter knew by revelation knowledge that Jesus really was the Christ and the Son of the living God. The Father revealed it to him by the Holy Spirit.

That is the best way I can explain what happened to me. I thank God for reaching out to me and showing me His loving-kindness. Maybe while you are reading this book, you too have a loved one who is blinded to the reality of Jesus. Let this be an encouragement to your faith—God can reach out to your loved one no matter where they are.

Ishmael and Saul

As we study Saul and the early Church, let us allow the Holy Spirit to paint a prophetic picture of Ishmael and today's Church.

The early Church was in the midst of great persecution. The foremost enemy of the Gospel was Saul, who even consented to the death of Stephen, causing believers in Christ to be scattered abroad over all Judea and Samaria (see Acts 8:1). Saul was an educated Hebrew, an Israelite from the tribe of Benjamin, and, as far as the law was concerned, he was a Pharisee (see Philippians 3:5). Saul ravaged the early Church with violence and cruelty. He went from house to house and dragged men and women and put them in prison for their belief in the Lord Jesus Christ (see Acts 8:3).

To complicate things further, he went to the high priest of that day with murderous intentions and threats against the disciples. He obtained warrants to go into the synagogues, arrest believers, and bring them back to Jerusalem for imprisonment. He was hostile and determined to put an end to what he considered blasphemy against God:

> *And Saul, yet breathing out threatenings and slaughter against the disciples of the Lord, went unto the high priest, And desired of him letters to Damascus to the synagogues, that if he found any of this way, whether they were men or women, he might bring them bound unto Jerusalem* (Acts 9:1-2).

Saul assumed his actions of violence toward the Church were of God. Yet he was, in reality, resisting the Son of God. He justified his attitude of pride and hatred for the disciples through the law that he was so well acquainted with. He knew the Scriptures but not the *One* who was spoken of in the Scriptures. He was driven by a zeal for God, yet was without knowledge of the truth. He thought he was serving the Lord; in reality, he was opposing.

Saul changed in a sudden encounter with the Lord Jesus on the road to Damascus. He saw the light of the glory of God and fell to the earth from which man was made, humbled by the majesty of God. His self-will was broken, his pride shattered, his zeal consumed, and his mind subdued by the glory of Jesus Christ. While on the ground, Saul heard the voice of the Master:

> *...Suddenly there shined round about him a light from heaven: And he fell to the earth, and heard a voice saying unto him, Saul, Saul, why persecutest thou me? And he said, Who art thou, Lord? And the Lord said, I am Jesus whom thou persecutest: it is hard for thee to kick against the pricks. And he trembling and astonished said, Lord, what wilt thou have me to do? And the Lord said unto him, Arise, and go into the city, and it shall be told thee what thou must do.*
>
> *And the men which journeyed with him stood speechless, hearing a voice, but seeing no man. And Saul arose from the earth; and when his eyes were opened, he saw no man: but they led him by the hand, and brought him into Damascus. And he was three days without sight, and neither did eat nor drink* (Acts 9:3-9).

At the feet of Jesus, Saul the murderer became Paul the martyr. His zeal for the law was consumed with a passion for Jesus

Christ. God had great purpose hidden in Paul, beyond what man could ever see. Paul was a chosen vessel for the Master's use in bearing the name of Jesus before Gentiles, kings, and all of Israel. Paul suffered much for the Gospel's sake but considered it a privilege to share the mysteries of the Gospel to a Gentile world.

Much of the Church today is afraid of Ishmael, as the early Church was afraid of Saul. Ishmael is wreaking havoc around the world and is the cause of much persecution to the Church, the Body of Christ. Television and the media are constantly bombarding us with stories of war, terrorism, and violence surrounding the Muslim world.

Saul was the foremost terrorist of his day.

In reality, not all Muslims are violent or terrorists, but there are certain elements of terrorism in Islam that will be discussed later in the book. Regardless, terrorism and Islam are synonymous in the world today. Saul was the foremost terrorist of his day. He threw stones instead of bombs, but his intent at heart was to destroy those he perceived to be the enemies of God. There are some among Ishmael doing the same today.

Muslims believe they are serving God in opposing the deity of Jesus Christ. An example: The Dome of the Rock dominates the skyline of Jerusalem, and, from the Muslim point of view, it is a symbol of Islam to the world. It is the third most holy site to Muslims, and the earliest monument celebrated by Muslims. First, they recognize it to be Mount Moriah, where Abraham offered Ishmael as a sacrifice—instead of Isaac. Second, they believe the prophet of Islam, Muhammad, ascended to Heaven from this rock in a night journey.

The dome is also a symbol of superiority before God—above Christians and Jews. Muslims believe they have the final and last revelation from God and sincerely oppose all others. To represent this attitude, the inscriptions and writings on the Dome of the Rock are passages from the Qur'an opposing the deity of Jesus, to let the world know that Jesus is not the Son of God. Muslims are sincere about their zeal for God, yet without knowledge of the truth. Just as Saul was the most unlikely candidate for the Kingdom, most would consider Ishmael to be the last to realize that Jesus is the Son of God.

Like Saul, Ishmael is about to have a head-on collision with the glory of the Lord Jesus Christ. The Father is about to show the face of Jesus to the Muslim people of the world. The Jesus they have opposed will become their Lord. (We will discuss how this shall be in Chapter 5.)

God has great purpose hidden in the Muslim people. Ishmael will be a chosen vessel in the hands of God. After God opens the eyes of Ishmael, He will use him for the purposes of the Kingdom. There is destiny camouflaged in the Muslim people yet to be seen. We see them like Saul, but God sees them like Paul—for such a time as this.

God is going to use the conversion of Ishmael to stir up the Church as He used the conversion of Saul to stir up the Church in the midst of persecution. The early Church was afraid of Saul in the hour of persecution, and all that heard of his conversion were amazed (Acts 9:21).

Likewise today, the Church will be amazed at the mass conversion of Ishmael. Even his own brethren in the flesh will be provoked to kill him, but Ishmael is not afraid of death or his enemies. Rather, this archer, once born of the Spirit, will be an arrow in the bow of God's hand shot into the heart of the enemy (satan) who once blinded him.

Jesus knows how to turn a murderer into a martyr for the Kingdom. There will be a holy fear of God and comfort of the Holy Ghost in the Church. The conversion of Ishmael will edify the Church and multiply it exceedingly. It will bring an awe and reverential fear of God to the Church. That is exactly what happened to the early Church (see Acts 9:31).

Also, God will use Ishmael to provoke the Church into a passion for Jesus. What the Church has forsaken, Ishmael will embrace. Ishmael has been in the desert, thirsty and hungry for fresh bread and living water. Once his eyes are opened, he will not hold back from the cause of Christ. Ishmael has been trained in the wilderness and is not afraid of his enemies. He will be grateful for Jesus the Messiah and count no cost too great to know the Master. Saul, the enemy of the Gospel, was transformed into Paul, the apostle, who wrote the following words inspired by the Holy Spirit:

> *I count all things but loss for the excellency of the knowledge of Christ Jesus my Lord: for whom I have suffered the loss of all things, and do count them but dung, that I may win Christ, And be found in him, not having mine own righteousness, which is of the law, but that which is through the faith of Christ, the righteousness which is of God by faith: That I may know him, and the power of his*

resurrection, and the fellowship of his sufferings, being made conformable unto his death (Philippians 3:8-10).

The passion that Ishmael will have for Jesus will be endless. His love for Jesus will be no secret and will be contagious to the Church. His passion for Jesus will provoke the Church to step out of complacency and familiarity of religion. Being provoked pricks our lukewarm hearts and allows us to look beyond false finish lines and comfort zones into the face of God. God provokes us to catch our attention and adjust our focus so that we may fix our eyes upon Jesus and what God is doing.

God is going to use Ishmael for His name's sake. He will suffer much, but he'll do it with pleasure and gladness. And He will use Ishmael to bear His name before Gentiles and kings and even Israel. It's a great work that God is going to do with Ishmael. There's destiny for the Muslim people, for God has not given up on them. God has not forgotten them; God has not forsaken them. They will not be termed forsaken or forgotten, or misunderstood or rejected or as terrorists; for God is going to change the face of Islam in the earth in this season, and you will not see the Muslim people as they were.

God will use Ishmael to provoke the Church into passion for Jesus.

But you will see them in the light of God's purpose for them, and you'll see them in the light of God's destiny. You will catch the heart of God and the impartation of His Spirit concerning these people, and you'll see them through the eyes of Jesus rather than the eyes of the world that has been painted for us through popular media.

It is important that we see the invisible and believe for the impossible. Ishmael will embrace his destiny and pursue the righteousness which is of God, through faith, rather than the righteousness of man, through works. His true identity in Christ will emerge. His zeal will be replaced by the power of God. The supernatural intervention of God among the Muslim people is very significant to the age we are living in. God has already begun this work, and we are hearing stories around the world of dynamic conversions of Muslims to Christ. We are about to see this happen to an entire generation of Muslims.

What the Church as forsaken,
Ishmael will embrace.

The Church and Ananias

Jesus appeared to Ananias in a vision concerning Saul's conversion:

And there was a certain disciple at Damascus, named Ananias; and to him said the Lord in a vision, Ananias. And he said, Behold, I am here, Lord. And the Lord said unto him, Arise, and go into the street which is called Straight, and inquire in the house of Judas for one called Saul, of Tarsus: for, behold, he prayeth, And hath seen in a

> *vision a man named Ananias coming in, and putting his hand on him, that he might receive his sight.*
>
> *Then Ananias answered, Lord, I have heard by many of this man, how much evil he hath done to thy saints at Jerusalem: And here he hath authority from the chief priests to bind all that call on thy name. But the Lord said unto him, Go thy way: for he is a chosen vessel unto me, to bear my name before the Gentiles, and kings, and the children of Israel: For I will show him how great things he must suffer for my name's sake* (Acts 9:10-16).

In a vision, Jesus told Ananias to go and pray for Saul of Tarsus so he could receive his sight. Ananias was astonished at the Lord's instructions and tried to convince the Lord of how evil Saul was. He sincerely reasoned with Jesus about the nuisance Saul had been to the believers in Christ. It was hard for Ananias to wrap his mind around the fact that God was asking him to go and pray for such a person.

Ananais was a faithful disciple; he was just being honest with the Lord. And we can be honest with the Lord; not condemning. We must be honest with him, and if we're being condemning, we need to have a heart-to-heart talk with Jesus and ask Him, "What's going on with the Muslim people?"

Jesus commanded Ananias to go and carry out his assignment while graciously revealing to him the greater purpose of God in choosing Saul. Jesus allowed Ananias to see Saul through God's eyes by telling him how Saul would bear the name of Jesus before Gentiles, kings, and all Israel for the glory of God.

God is opening our eyes
to see Ishmael in light of His purpose.

I believe the Church is in a similar place concerning the Muslim people. The reputation of Ishmael in the world is one of war, violence, and terrorism. The Church has only seen Ishmael as Abraham's mistake and a work of the flesh that we have to live with. Like Ananias, God is opening our eyes to see Ishmael in light of His purpose. The Lord is not willing that *any* perish (2 Pet. 3:9), and He is unveiling the destiny of the Muslim people.

You may be reading this today and wondering how this could be. Or Jesus may be speaking to you about your role in this *kairos* moment for the Muslim people. You may have a burden for them and the need to be in your prayer closet interceding for them as a whole or even individually. It is important to know your role in this marvelous harvest. I believe that, as we continue through the ninth chapter of the Book of Acts, we will find the answer to our function as the Church, the Body of Christ, in this hour:

> *And Ananias went his way, and entered into the house; and putting his hands on him said, Brother Saul, the Lord, even Jesus, that appeared unto thee in the way as thou camest, hath sent me, that thou mightest receive thy sight, and be filled with the Holy Ghost. And immediately there fell from his eyes as it had been scales: and he received sight forthwith, and arose, and was baptized. And when he had received meat, he was strengthened* (Acts 9:17-19).

Obedience is the first step. The key is to hear what the Spirit is saying and obey. The Holy Spirit will challenge our limitations with revelation in the Word of God and illuminate our understanding. Ananias carried out the instructions of the Lord and saw the results; the Church must do the same.

Today's Church is like Ananias.

Alignment

This is the time we're living in. The Saul of our day is Ishmael, and the Church is like Ananais. And we must deal with these things, and bring alignment. Kingdom alignment precedes kingdom assignment. We must come into alignment with God's greater purpose, so that our unique assignments in the Body can be set and fulfilled.

Is it about how many Muslims are in your city? Not necessarily. This is a global issue; this is a national thing. It doesn't matter how many Muslims are in your city. It's about God's heart. It's about His people. He didn't say the Lord is willing that none shall perish only if they're in your city. What about the other cities, what about the other nations, what about the other people?

You must expand...until now we've had a "fishing-pole mentality." And if you notice in the Gospels, many times that's how they fished. We know how to be fishers of men, and that's good, don't give that up—we need to have a fisherman mentality. But we're moving into a season of harvest where we need to have a *net* mentality.

Jesus is saying to the Church, cast your nets on the right side of the boat. Maybe you have not seen a harvest, maybe you've gone all these years and maybe you've been in darkness and you've not seen the harvest you'd like to have seen in the Muslim world. Jesus is telling us to cast our nets, to do the unconventional thing which you think is impossible.

Jesus says:

> At my command and because this is the right season and because I'm standing here and saying to you to do it, cast your nets on the right side of the boat and there will be a multitude of harvest of fish, a multitude of harvest of people, that you will not be able to carry the nets to shore and bring them to me.
>
> You're going to have to call on your brethren and the other Churches, and all of them will be working together. All will come together for one common cause, the sake of the harvest of the nations, for the sake of the harvest of the Muslim people, for the sake of the harvest of humanity. And bring them together by the instruction of the Spirit of the Lord, for there is a divine grace, a pre-eminent grace, in this time and this season to see souls won supernaturally by the power of the Spirit of God! And it shall be. It shall be.

God said to me that a whole generation of Muslims will come into the Kingdom of God. The average age of the world's Muslim population is under the age of 35. Most of them are under 30 years of age. In other words, more than a billion Muslims are younger than that age bracket. Do not take for granted the young population.

For example, young people in France are disillusioned. Many of the Muslim immigrants live in one particular suburb, and they are becoming disillusioned because the young people are in the midst of a crisis because of what God is doing there. There's a crisis in Islam. The young people are asking, "What is this Islam? This religion and these rules and this terrorism—is this what Islam really is?"

There is a great temptation, and it is a great desire of the enemy to graft the young people, recruit them into terrorism, because they have no hope or direction. The enemy tempts them into violence, problems, and all kinds of terror because in that environment they find cause and purpose. Young Muslims are told that if they do this thing and die, or commit *Jihad* and die in the Holy War, they will go to go to Heaven because God will be pleased with them.

Otherwise they will have to please God by works, then they can have 72 virgins. So many young Muslims have no one to believe in them. They're disillusioned, and they believe they have an option to go to Heaven. They are in the valley of decision.

Because a majority of Muslims are under the age of 35, the enemy is trying to thwart the plan of God. Whenever God has a destiny for a person, a people, a nation, or a Church, the enemy comes in its infancy to thwart His plan. That's why the Church must come together and protect the plan of God that's coming forth. We must unite so we can become a greater force together.

How Shall This Be?

Before I asked the Father, "How shall this be?" He asked me a question that surprised me.

I was walking in my living room, and He said, "Will you go to these my people?" I didn't even know why He called them His people until I began to see some of these things. By creation, all are His people. But by destiny God looks at the future and calls them His people—He calls things that are not as though they are, because that's the way our God is (Isa. 46:10). God does not live in time, He lives in eternity where there's no time—it is all *now*.

That's why when you go to Heaven you hear "Holy, Holy, Holy, the whole earth *is filled* with the Lord's glory." (See Isaiah 6:3.) When we rise up to a place into a spiritual height where God is, we begin to see the world as He sees it. When we see it, it shall be as He sees it and as He decrees and declares it—as we align ourselves with Him. God is saying something about the Muslim people. He began to speak to me from His heart about their purpose. Now back to my response:

I said, "Lord, I don't want to be like Peter, as far as I know I'll do anything you tell me to do."

And then He began to open my heart and speak to me and show me His heart and plan for these people. He showed me that the Church must stand in the gap for Ishmael. There are things that are going to happen in the endtimes, and yes, there is going to be wrath and judgment. But there's still a time of mercy right now. This is an urgent season when the Church needs to move out and share God's mercy with them.

He said to me, "Many have been afraid of them and many whom I've called and sent have been afraid and backed away. Will you go to these my people?" It is God's heart for them; I felt His love for them. It was so much more than I imagined He could have for these people. It was so genuine, so close to Him. And the picture I had of them and the experience I had as a Muslim was very foreign to this. But God's heart was full of love.

And I said, "God, as far as I know, I'll go."

During the conversation I had with God about how it shall be, He gave me five things He's going to do in this hour to cooperate with the Church so the multitude of harvest can be realized. I will detail those five things and then say something about the overall strategy that I see God using.

1. Spiritual Wall

The first thing He told me: there is *a wall in the spirit* that has kept the gospel from the Muslim people. He likened the wall to a two-leafed gate, a strong, ancient gate that kings used to hide their treasures behind. It was made of iron, covered with brass, and it had a lock on it. Nobody could go in, it was closed, and it was guarded. God said to me that we've moved into a season when He is opening the two-leafed gates that have kept the gospel out of the nation of Islam in masses. He said, "I am causing the wall of Islam to come down, and the Church must be ready and prepare for this harvest. Just like the wall of communism fell down; the wall of Islam shall fall." And in the Spirit He said, "I'll have you know, it has already fallen. It is yet to be seen in the natural, and it will become common knowledge soon."

So that is part of the reason why it was so difficult for years to reach Muslims with the gospel. God is now saying, "I will go before you. I will go before the Church. I'm opening the way; the gates won't be shut." He's going to open them, and He said that the people will come out, and the secret treasures hidden in darkness will also appear. But we must go to the people. That's the first thing He spoke to me about how it shall be.

2. Media

The second thing He spoke to me about was strategy—about *media*. He said, "I will use media profusely. That means television, satellite, Internet, radio, every way of communicating—film, whatever you can." God will use any and all methods of communication to reach His people. The Church is going to personally go to people, but there will be something beyond that. God said He is going to use television and media in masses over the Muslim world globally. Television and media will find invitation and entrance through key "pharaohs" in the Muslim world into the Muslim nations.

God is going to give media and television favor, and He said He's going to use them. That is one of the reasons my wife and I have answered the call to media. We believe that Kingdom media is a key platform that God will use to reach the masses. This is not the only one, but it is an important one. God gave me a Scripture about this, exactly how He was going to use television, the strategy of television and media. It is found in Acts 10:44, "*While Peter yet spake these words, the Holy Ghost fell on all them which heard the word.*"

He said that while men and women are yet speaking, the Holy Spirit will fall on them who hear the Word. Can you imagine a Muslim family sitting in their home and watching television? They tune in to our program (mostly because I have a Muslim name) and watch the show. Can you imagine that family watching, and the Spirit of God falling on them and filling them with the Holy Spirit? And they start praying in tongues and saying that Jesus is Lord? That's a pretty good way to bring people to Christ.

That's what happened in Acts 10:44 at Cornelius' house. This is a scriptural precedent. There is something great about our Father; He is a God of exceeding greatness. That means He just can't do less than what He did before. That means whatever He does will always exceed in greatness more than He did before.

Let me share a testimony with you about God's strategy using media. A gentleman recorded a portion of our television program onto his cell phone—he recorded a little bit of my testimony. Then he invited his best friend, who is a Muslim, to his house. He showed him the cell phone and played the television testimony for him to see. The presence of God came into the room, and the Muslim gives his heart to Jesus. He is now attending Church.

God's presence penetrates.

The guy called me and told me what happened. I was excited, I had never thought of using a cell phone like that! He said, "I walked in, saw the show, put it on my cell phone, and went, and the person got saved." After that he used a bunch of videos, tools, and books from us, and he's lead many Muslim people to the Lord in Ontario.

I'm telling you the day has come; if you're asking a question as even the prophets asked, "Shall a nation be born at once?" (Isa. 66:8). Shall a land be changed in a day? I say to you the answer is "Yes." That nation is the Muslim nation, the nation of Islam.

Meaning, in a short period of time there will be such a move. It's going to startle and marvel the world. The secular world will take interest of it, and they will say, "Wow, whoever this Father is who would be willing to reach for such a people as this, the people who we think the worst of—I want to know who this Father is!"

It will awaken a cry in that generation because there are a lot of young people, a whole generation, who are rebellious and think they are forsaken. They feel lost and say, I want to know who this God is. God has purpose in this television and media strategy.

Muslims pay close attention to revelation knowledge because their entire concept of the Qur'an is based on *Wahi* which means "revelation or revealed." They believe the Qur'an was revealed to Muhammad, the prophet of Islam, by the angel Gabriel. They pay careful attention to revelation. So when God began to deal with me deeper about Acts 10:44, He said, "The life and revelation of My Word will proceed over the airwaves while you are yet speaking, while men and women are yet speaking, meaning speaking by the Spirit of God."

John 1:4, *"In Him was life; and the life was the light of men,"* was the reputation of Jesus. You can have light, which is knowledge and truth, but if you have no *life*, what distances you from other religions? Everybody's got light and knowledge—me as a Muslim had light and knowledge. But the Bible warns us in Luke

11:35, *"take heed therefore that the light which is in thee be not darkness."*

And Matthew 6:23 says, *"if therefore the light that is in thee be darkness, how great is that darkness!"* So just having light, knowledge, and illumination is not enough. We must have the *life* of God which is a privilege of them who believe in Jesus.

We have the life abiding inside us, and we're connected to the true vine which is Jesus. (See John 15:5.) We are reaping the Spirit of God which is the life feeding us. That is "speaking by revelation." I don't mean speaking by information, for there has been much information that has puffed up the minds of people. This is an hour of revelation when the Spirit of revelation shall come upon the Church, and the Spirit of wisdom will declare forth the wisdom of God to the intent that principalities and powers will see the wisdom of our God.

Revelation has to go forth; the life of God has to go forth! But God wants revelation that is the key to what's going to happen. It's illumination of their revelation. Illumination light is OK, but *illumination* means it is "shining forth *from* something—a source." It's got to be illuminating from the life of Jesus; then it will be a light to all who are lost in darkness.

3. Dreams and Visions

The third thing God shared with me when I asked Him, "How shall this be?" *was dreams and visions.*

I believe God is saying, "I'm going to give dreams and visions of Jesus to the Muslim people. They will see a man clothed in white, with holes in His hands, and He's going to say, 'I am the way, the truth and the life.' They'll want to know who that man is."

As you read in the previous chapter, they will go knocking on the door of the mosque, at their business places, in the marketplace, and then they will come to the Church and ask, "Who is this Man? I can't get Him out of my consciousness. He has arrested me."

And the Church will be able to say, "This is Jesus!"

God gave Pharaoh a dream that left him restless in search of the truth. The dream so gripped his consciousness that he sought out Joseph from prison to understand the truth (Genesis 41:14). There are men like Pharaoh in the business world and in governments of the Islamic world who God is going to reach through dreams and visions of Jesus. They will be key instruments in creating platforms for the Gospel to reach behind closed doors. Joseph was prepared in the Holy Spirit to access the wisdom of God, and we as the Church must be prepared and positioned to move with God. Maybe you have been in prison with an unfulfilled dream, deprived of your destiny, but God is about to bring you out into a wealthy place where your gift will be in demand by the Pharaohs of the world. For that which you have been prepared for all your life is about to manifest before you. God is speaking to people through dreams and visions of Jesus to get their attention.

God is speaking through
dreams and visions of Jesus.

We are living in a dispensation of the new covenant where God is putting the law into the minds and hearts of people (Jeremiah 31:33). The Holy Spirit, speaking through Peter, reminds us of the Word of the Lord:

> *And it shall come to pass in the last days, saith God, I will pour out of my Spirit upon all flesh: and your sons and your daughters shall prophesy, and your young men shall see visions, and your old men shall dream dreams: And on my servants and on my handmaidens I will pour out in those days of my Spirit; and they shall prophesy* (Acts 2:17-18).

God says in the Book of Acts and in Joel 2:28-29, "I'll pour out my Spirit upon all flesh. Young men shall see visions and old men shall dream dreams. Your handmaidens and children will prophesy." Is it a way of God to show visions and dreams to unbelievers? Absolutely! Pharaoh had a dream in the time of Joseph. He was caught up with restlessness; the dream gripped his consciousness and arrested him.

Let me give you an example of a Muslim who was transformed by a vision of Jesus. A Muslim lady called us from Alberta one day. She said that she had been praying and praying and one day she just cried out to Jesus, and He appeared in her room. She gave her heart to Jesus. She told her husband about it, and he left her and took the two children with him. Her two children were eventually returned to her, but then her brother-in-law threatened to kill her for her decision to accept Christ.

She called and said, "I'm not afraid because I know Jesus! They can't touch me, because I know Jesus' truth and He's the way and the life, and He's my Lord. I'm not afraid of what they're saying to me. Can you help me find a Church? Can you help me go to a Church? Please, I need to go to a Church."

My wife, who ministers especially to Muslim women, spoke to her. My wife asked her, "Have you received the Holy Ghost?"

"I haven't even heard of the Holy Ghost," the woman said. She was just loving and trusting Jesus because she had a vision and a dream.

I searched and was happy when I found one in her city that told me they had a ministry to Muslim women. I was excited that this Church seemed to be ready for the harvest. Then they told me that they had a "craft ministry" for Muslim women.

"A craft ministry? This situation is beyond a craft ministry. They're trying to kill this woman right now and kill her children, and she doesn't care. She loves Jesus, and she wants the Word. She's willing to go out there and preach the gospel and be martyred if she has to. She's willing to do everything that Jesus said. She just needs some help, someone to teach her."

I'm not opposed to the craft ministry by the way, but we have to understand the seriousness of these days. Did Jesus say go ye into all the world, preach the Gospel of the Kingdom of Heaven, lay hands on the sick, cast out devils, raise the dead...and make crafts wherever you go? We must graduate from Crafts 101 and be able to minister to them the life of God. That's going to take some training and equipping.

There are two things that the Church must pray. Number one, the Church must pray that God would reawaken the cry that is resident in the Muslim heart. How will the cry be awakened? As revelation and life of His Word by the Spirit of God goes forth, it will unleash the cry that has been birthed in the prayer chamber of His glory, by them who pray and intercede and yield themselves to the Spirit of God.

As that prayer is answered, the second thing you must pray is that God would open the eyes of Ishmael that he might see Jesus and know who He is. Strategic prayer is better than general prayer—general prayer may step you up and lead you to strategic prayer, but strategic prayer will get you to the place of victory.

Prayer is like surfing, the surfboard is made of the Word of God. You begin to surf on the waves of the Holy Spirit, based on having a surfboard. If you don't have the Word to surf with, it's going to be hard to surf on the waters of the Spirit.

With the Word of God as the board beneath your feet, you can surf every wave, even the higher and bigger ones, and you can adventurously pray in the Holy Ghost and get things done. Key strategies and revelation are important.

We have pastors who call us all the time, and tell us that Muslims come to their Church and get saved, and they start reading the Bible two or three hours a day every morning—and the pastor never told them to do so. They say to the pastor, "We go to work at our job at 9 a.m. So we get up at 5 in the morning and read our Bible for 2½ hours, husband and wife together."

The pastor asks them, "Why?"

The response: "Well remember when you preached on tithing? I thought if I'm going to tithe to the Lord from my money, why don't I give Him of my time also."

Then they ask many questions about the Word that the pastor can't answer. These pastors call me, and I don't know the answers either because their mind-set is different, they're coming from a different place, and their questions are linked and geared from a different place. There has to be some training and equipping to be able to deal with issues that new-believer Muslims present. And that's one of the reasons why we started our ministry.

Another pastor told me about a Muslim man who had a dream for several nights in a row. Some are having literal dreams and encounters with Jesus. but some are seeing symbolic things that start the journey that arrests their attention to look for Jesus. Either way it's God's decision how He wants to will it by His Spirit to have it done. This Muslim man was looking for the answers to his dream, so he went to the Church door, knocked, and told the pastor that he had some questions for him. They sat down, and he shared his dream with the pastor.

He said, "I have this dream where I see a huge high fence, and I begin to climb the fence. As I climb the fence I get up a little bit, and then I fall to the ground. Then I get up. I climb the fence again, and I fall to the ground. I keep doing this, and I'm getting frustrated. I know I must get to the other side of the fence, but I can't because I keep falling to the ground. I need to get to the other side, and I don't know how. I know this dream is from God, and I know God is trying to speak to me. Could you help me interpret what this means?"

The Spirit of God gave the pastor the interpretation, and he said, "You are trying to get to the other side which is Heaven, and you're trying to do it by your own works. That's why you keep falling to the ground, because you're not good enough to get there on your own works. But you can get to Heaven through the grace of the Lord Jesus Christ."

He shared the Gospel with him and the Muslim told him to wait a moment. He left and returned with five of his Muslim friends—all of them were born again, baptized, and now attend the Church. We have story after story like this coming into our offices. And now they are coming not just nationally, but also globally.

Statistically, around the world now, the number one way a Muslim comes to Jesus is by a dream or a vision; and I want to declare this to you: *those instances will increase.* Isn't that interesting that that is the supernatural sovereignty of God and power of God? It is not a works thing on our part. *We just have to cooperate with the Spirit of God.* He's the one who is going to make it happen. We have testimony after testimony of these types of exciting things happening.

And not just Muslims call us; Hindus call too. God is after all the nations. He is after all Gentiles. A Hindu lady called and said she walked into her house, and a man was in the living room clothed in white with bright lights, sitting on the couch. As she looked at the man the fear of the Lord came on her, and she doesn't know what to do. She was startled and walked out the door. Then she ran back in, and He was gone. She knew it was Jesus.

"I need Jesus."

And so she went around town—notice the innocence—for four months wandering, looking for this person named Jesus, because she didn't understand. "Where's this person Jesus? I need Jesus." And she finally came to a place where she saw a Cross, and thought that this had something to do with Jesus. She went home and cried out to God saying, "Jesus where are you? I've looked for you; I've searched for you. I went everywhere. I can't find you. Jesus, where are you?"

And Jesus appeared in the room, took her hands, and she was healed of sickness. She gave her heart to Jesus, and then she led 70 of her family members to the Lord. She's born again and on fire for God.

These are all recent happenings. This next report from Egypt, was actually televised on Egyptian television and was banned in the Muslim world. A missionary shared it with me, and I'm just going to share it with you anyway. A Muslim man killed his wife, buried her, and also buried alive their two daughters. One daughter was 8 years old, and the other daughter was a nursing baby. He buried them and left. Fifteen days later an uncle died, and when they came to bury the uncle in the same grave, they found the two daughters alive. This caused a huge commotion.

Then an anchor woman wearing a burka (only her eyes were visible) interviewed the 8-year-old daughter on Egyptian television. The girl was asked how she stayed alive every day, what had happened?

The girl responded, "Every morning a man clothed in white came. He had holes in His hands, and He woke my mother so she could feed my baby sister. He would bring me food every day."

The interviewer said, "That sounds like this man named Jesus we've been hearing about, and if He's got holes in His hands maybe He really died as they say..." Then they cut the feed, and the television went blank. Now the girls can't be found, and this has been part of the challenge about getting this story out. People want to air this story, but they can't yet because they're looking for the girls who haven't been found. The story has been documented as far as many people heard the story. Some heard it on radio; some saw it on television. I personally heard this from missionaries from Egypt who I know and trust, as well as from several other missionaries and other ministers.

A Man in white fed us every day.

Jesus is the resurrection and life. Jesus has his own reputation in the Middle East. It's amazing. The Church has one reputation in the world, but Jesus has His own reputation in the Middle East. Mind you, it should be the same. It should be, and bless God it will be one day. Amen. It shall be; it shall come to pass.

4. The Glory of God

The fourth thing He said to me was that the glory of God, the *Kabod* of God, was going to be manifest among the Muslim people and among the nations, the Gentiles. Now understand, God is not a respecter of persons, what He'll do for one He'll do for another. God's heart is for all the nations, for all Gentile people, for the Church. He loves the Church, and He loves the nation of Israel. We're going to get into all of that later in the book, but God is interested in the harvest of all souls. Now, He is focusing and triggering on Muslims because He knows that will stir up a harvest in the nations—He's wise about the way.

To win souls you have to be wise. To be a fisher of men you have to learn from the master. He knows how to fish and He's about to cast His net to bring in that harvest. The glory of God must manifest. Isn't it awesome what Jesus is doing around the world? It is a supernatural thing, don't put pressure on yourself. Let the Holy Spirit do it.

The cell phone story? That was the Holy Ghost. No man could do that. Use a cell phone for a few minutes, and then have it save someone—that was the awesome glory of God. Isaiah chapter 60 contains an important principle about the glory; it reveals why the glory is so key.

> *Arise, shine for thy light has come and the glory of the Lord has risen upon you. For behold the* ***darkness*** *shall cover the earth and* ***gross darkness*** *the people, but the Lord shall arise on you and His glory shall be seen upon thee* (Isaiah 60:1, emphasis added).

What is the difference between darkness and gross darkness? When you don't have the lights on in a room; that's darkness. You turn the lights on when the gospel is preached; people can see. Light comes, and they hear the Gospel. But *gross darkness* prevents a person from seeing Jesus even though the lights are on and the gospel is around. God has an answer to darkness and gross darkness. Light takes care of darkness, but the glory of God takes care of gross darkness. This is why people get concerned when they look at the world's condition or the condition of a nation and see evil. God's got a plan.

> The glory of God destroys gross darkness.

Certain things will not be handled without the glory of God. That's why the glory must manifest—so those greater things can be done. Certain greater works are limited to the greater glory and the manifestation of His glory. Light takes care of darkness; the glory of God takes care of gross darkness. And that's a real key when we're praying. Now imagine a Muslim fellow watching television, and suddenly the glory of God comes into his room, falls on him, and he finds out who Jesus is. What a great thing to have happen! He might want to throw his shoe at the television, but right then the power of God comes into his room.

5. Miracles, Signs, and Wonders

The fifth thing God shared with me is miracles, signs, and wonders. Arms are going to grow back; legs are going to grow back; dead are going to be raised, and we will see tremendous power over witchcraft. Muslims don't have an answer for witchcraft. They don't know how to deal with it. But the power of Jesus over the power of darkness is a great testimony to the Muslim people.

We've had many experiences of that with our ministry. Especially when we went to Pakistan and saw God's power manifest over witchdoctors. That kind of power is key; we need that power. We need that glory to come down—the glory of God. With no fight, no war; the glory of God came down, and it was over. That's why we need the glory of God.

Miracles, signs, and wonders are also keys to what God is doing in the earth realm. Muslims have trouble with the idea of resurrecting the dead, because they know that the only person who can raise the dead is Jesus. They believe that God exclusively gave that power to Jesus—that's what they believe. So that's why they believe in Jesus' ministry, by the way. Jesus performed miracles and caused people to rise from the dead. To them, seeing miracles or resurrection power points to Jesus. If this is happening, they wonder why because only Jesus can do this. And furthermore they wonder, how can someone in the name of Jesus do this thing. So the demonstration of resurrection power can be a great witness to the Muslim.

There is a realm of the supernatural above the earthly politics and red tape of ministry. This is the realm of miracles, signs, and wonders. It involves more than just knowing the acts of God, but also the ways of God. The children of Israel knew the acts of God yet died in the wilderness. Moses knew the ways of God and saw His glory.

It is about living in the realm of Heaven and visiting earth rather than living on earth and visiting Heaven. It is not a realm of visitation, but a realm of habitation. It is a realm where you see earth through the eyes of Heaven. It is a realm of faith where you see the invisible and do the impossible. It is a realm where you no longer follow the acts of God, but where the acts of God follow you. It is a state of being where you are not just *under* the cloud of God, but *in* the cloud of God. It not just about *seeing* the pillar of fire by night but it is about *being* the pillar of fire by night in Christ Jesus. His ministers ought to be flames of fire. It is not just about the miracles, but it is about the Spirit in which you live, move, and have your being.

Man has always asked God to come down to where he is, but God is asking us to come up to where He is. God comes to the place where we are, but there is a higher place in the Spirit where He is. This is the realm we are born of and destined to live and walk in. In this realm we breathe the presence of God and manifest the life of God. In this realm, we are not impressed by miracles but are rather in awe of the majesty of God. It is not just the outer court where we hear the Word, or the inner court where we walk in the Word, but the Holy of Holies where we become the Word. It is where we become living epistles read of all men.

We are living in an hour when God is raising up a generation that will speak as the oracle of God while in the cloud of glory. It is not a realm of enticing words of man's wisdom, but a realm of demonstration and power of the Holy Ghost. While Philip was yet preaching, demons left people. (See Acts 8:6-7.)

It is a realm where devils tremble and flee rather than fight. It is a realm of the glory of God. It is a realm where we are *not*, and Jesus *is*. It is a secret place where your identity is hidden in Christ alone. It is a realm where man can no longer be seen because all that is seen is the glory of God. It is a realm where man cannot deny the existence and majesty of God. The whole earth shall be covered with the glory of God as the waters cover the sea. The density of God's presence will be immeasurable, and the lightning of God will flash through the souls of men.

Jesus said, preach the Kingdom of Heaven, it is at hand, cast out devils, cleanse the lepers, and raise the dead—freely you have received, freely give (Matt. 10:8). There's a dimension of that kind of power coming, and when the glory of God manifests that way, there are also sensitive things to be careful about. Once the glory is revealed and manifested, the same glory that could raise someone from the dead can also cause someone to drop dead. Being bold and true, I must tell you that both will actually happen.

The Role of the Church

So those are the five major aspects of how He is going to cooperate with the Church. Concerning the Church's role, let's go back to Acts chapter 9 and gather more insight as to why God wants to bring the Muslim people into His Kingdom. There is more to His purpose in naming Ishmael before he was born. Not only does he want to awaken their cry and show them the face of Jesus so they can see the Father, but He also wants to use Ishmael to provoke the Church.

The Church was progressing fine, but God used Saul of Tarsus (Paul when he was converted) to provoke the Church. Why? To provoke the Church into a passion for Christ. God is going to use Ishmael to provoke the Church into a passion for Jesus Christ. For what the Church is forsaking in Jesus, Ishmael will embrace. He has been thirsty in the wilderness for 4,000 years, and when he gets a sip of the living water, when he gets a taste of the living bread, he's never going to be the same. He's going to begin to do what that Word says, and he's going to provoke the Church.

Being provoked
pricks lukewarm hearts.

Is provoking good? Yes. In the New Testament it says provoke one another unto good works and love. (See Hebrews 10:24.) So there's a holy provoking that can occur too. Why is provoking necessary? Because when God provokes us, He gets our attention and causes us to focus away from lukewarm, false finish lines. He is going to use Ishmael to provoke the Church.

When you see a more than a hundred Muslims who are on fire for God show up in your Church, it'll provoke you. It will provoke you when and they say, "We led 12 people to the Lord this week and they're asking so many questions—what do we do next?" It's going to provoke you when they tell you that they prayed for someone, and his arms grew out.

Now what?

Or they might say to you, "We've got a problem. We didn't know the laws about desecrating the dead, so we raised this guy from the dead—what do we do now?"

Will that provoke anybody? When these new believers tell us about having encounters with Jesus we will probably think, "Hold on, Jesus, we have to have a talk with you for a moment. We've been around for 20 years, and I haven't had these kinds of encounters with you."

It's going to get our attention, it's going to cause us to break and rend our hearts so much so that we cry out to Him, "Jesus, I want you. Jesus, I need you. Jesus, I have to be with you. I have to see You, have to know You, have to hear You. I have to know your Word!"

Suddenly everything else will not be a priority, and Jesus will become the single focus of your life—that's where passion is birthed. When your vision and eye is single-minded and focused upon Jesus, it will birth a light and a passion in the whole body.

The Comforter

He is also going to use Ishmael to bring the Church comfort in the Holy Ghost and return the fear of the Lord to the Church. When Saul of Tarsus became Paul, the Bible says that the people of God were edified, comforted, and they reverenced the Lord. (See Acts 9:31.) Ishmael is going to be used...Ishmael is a chosen vessel unto Jesus in these times, and He is going to use him. And He has a plan for him. It's going to start with the Church letting the Holy Spirit adjust our hearts and our mindset concerning these people—seeing them through the eyes of Jesus, in the light of their purpose.

It will take prayer and intercession from a genuine heart, raising them up to God so God can open their eyes. What is it to you if God opens their eyes? I didn't say *you* are going to open their eyes; in fact, quit trying to open their eyes, let the Spirit of God open them.

When I was a Muslim, I was adamantly opposed to the gospel, no person could have convinced me that Jesus is the Son of God. In fact, I was trying to convert Christians to Islam. But then I had an encounter with the living God. In a moment, I was no longer a Muslim who didn't know Jesus as the Son of God—I came to the revelation of the son of the living God. I had more than faith; I knew it with all my heart. My life was transformed on July 3,

1994, when I gave my life to Christ. I had an encounter, a head-on collision with the glory of God.

The Muslim people are in for a head-on collision with the glory and the majesty of our God. How majestic is our God! How glorious is our God! Church, are you ready for this hour? Are you ready for this *kairos* season? Are you ready for what God is about to do in the world on a global scale?

Are you ready?

Meditation Moment

Consider the five strategies that God has planned to bring about the Muslim harvest. Are you surprised? Has your understanding about God's love for all people been deepened? Can the Body of Christ move past "craft ministries" to "saving ministries" for those Muslims who are putting their lives on the line in Jesus' name?

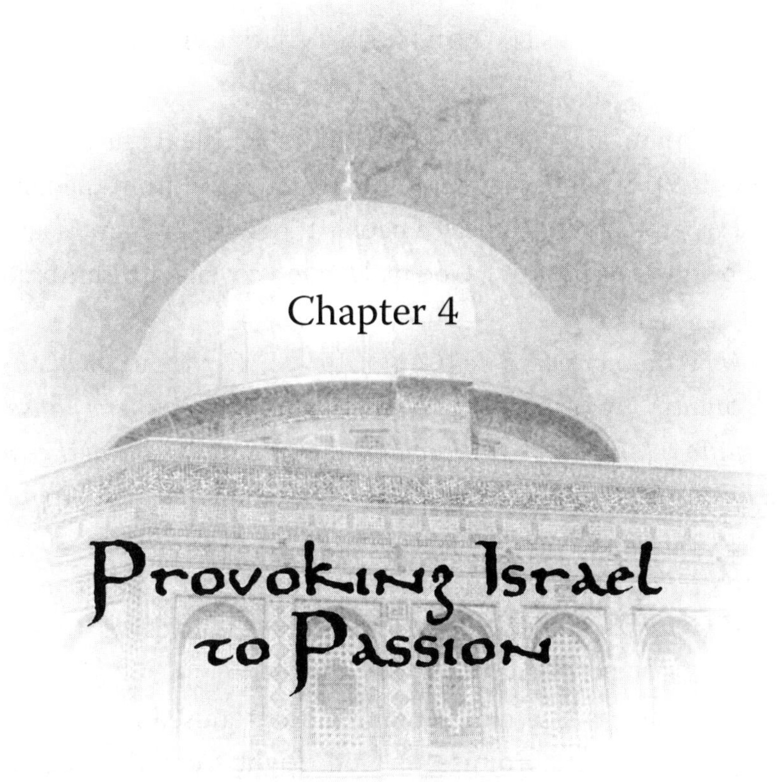

Chapter 4

Provoking Israel to Passion

THE almighty God of Heaven and earth is not a respecter of persons—He loves all. God is love and the Father of lights. *All nations are made of one blood and redeemed through the blood of One, Jesus Christ.* However, not all in the earth have become partakers of this redemption. God in the New Testament recognizes humanity in three groups of people: Jews, Gentiles (nations), and the Church (Body of Christ):

> *Give none offence, neither to the Jews, nor to the Gentiles, nor to the Church of God* (1 Corinthians 10:32).

He loves all of them and has a plan for all of them. Our Heavenly Father wills that none should perish and that all would come to salvation in Christ Jesus. Going back to the days of Noah, we see that, after the flood, Noah replenished the earth (see Genesis 9). Noah gave birth to the nations; and from the nations, God separated unto Himself a people through Abraham, Isaac, and Jacob known as the Jews. God had made a covenant with Abraham:

> *Now the Lord had said unto Abram, Get thee out of thy country, and from thy kindred, and from thy father's house, unto a land that I will show thee: And I will make of thee a great nation, and I will bless thee, and make thy name great; and thou shalt be a blessing: And I will bless them that bless thee, and curse him that curseth thee: and in thee shall all families of the earth be blessed* (Genesis 12:1-3).

Abraham had no children and God promised he would have seed to fulfill the promise of God. Right from the beginning, God's intention in separating a Jewish people was to eventually bless the families of the earth. God's long-term plan was for the Gentiles to come into the Kingdom in due order. "*In Isaac shall thy seed be called*" (Gen. 21:12) was the promise of God to Abraham and likewise to Isaac concerning Jacob. Then Jacob became Israel, the father of the 12 tribes of Israel.

In essence, God separated a people unto Himself so that, through their seed, He could bless the rest of the peoples of the earth. For centuries there were two groups of people on the earth: Jews and Gentiles. The Jews were blessed and partakers of God's covenant. The Gentiles were strangers to the covenants and promises of Israel, without God in the earth (see Ephesians 2:12).

God will seek them who are no people.

On the Cross, God took away the middle wall of partition between Jew and Gentile, allowing all who would believe on Jesus to become one Body in Christ Jesus. This group is made of all humankind: Jews and Gentiles (nations) alike, transformed into a new creature in Christ Jesus who is Messiah to the Jew, Savior to the world, and Lord to the Church. We are stones fitly joined together into one Body of the Lord Jesus Christ.

To the Jewish people, the most noticeable of the Gentiles is Ishmael, because he was cast out of Abraham's house and left with no inheritance and no chance to ever be an heir. He was left to remain the son of a servant named Hagar:

> *Wherefore she said unto Abraham, Cast out this bondwoman and her son: for the son of this bondwoman shall not be heir with my son, even with Isaac* (Genesis 21:10).

Israel takes pride in the very fact that God separated unto Himself Abraham from the nations, Isaac from Ishmael, and Jacob from Esau. The Jewish people are secure in knowing that God, by election, chose Isaac, the father of Jacob (Israel), over Ishmael, the son of the bondwoman. Ishmael was born of the flesh and, upon mocking Isaac, was cast out from the law, the promises, and the covenants of Israel. The Muslims today surround Israel and yet are considered no people, from a covenant perspective, to the Jewish people.

You might wonder why Ishmael was cast out in the first place? In the beginning when Sarah was pregnant, Ishmael's mother left; but the angel of the Lord told her to go back to her mistress. Suddenly Ishmael is all grown up, and God tells Abraham to let him go.

Why was Ishmael cast out? Why did God allow that to happen? The answer is found in Galatians 4:21-31—Ishmael is symbolic of the law. When Isaac, the promise came, the law had to go. That's why in the New Testament when Jesus came, the law vanishes.

There had to be a type and a shadow in the Old Testament according to Hebrews 10:1, so it could be fulfilled in the New Testament. The law that cast him out, will be replaced with the grace of Jesus Christ that will bring him in.

This is the time in which we are living.

Jealousy and Anger

God spoke by the prophet Moses concerning Israel:

> *They have moved me to jealousy with that which is not God; they have provoked me to anger with their vanities: and I will move them to jealousy with those which are not a people; I will provoke them to anger with a foolish nation.* (Deuteronomy 32:21).

In biblical days, Israel provoked God to jealousy by going after strange gods. Israel went after gods who were not God, and likewise, God will go after them who are not his chosen people. Israel took foolish idols to anger God; likewise God will take a foolish nation to anger Israel. The Bible says "*no people,*" meaning a people of no covenant with God, strangers to the promises of God made to Israel. Romans 11:11 says that through the salvation of the Gentiles, Israel is provoked to jealousy.

There is no greater Gentile to provoke Israel to jealousy than Ishmael, nor a more foolish nation to anger Israel than Islam. The Muslims are the least likely people in the eyes of Israel to be worthy of salvation and God's outstretched hand of goodness. As far as Israel is concerned, Ishmael is still mocking them in war, violence, and terrorism. Ishmael is the last person Israel expects God to reach out to.

Ishmael was cast out for Isaac's sake, but God will bring him into the Kingdom for Israel's sake.

The law of God they so diligently serve cast out Ishmael with no inheritance, making him a stranger to the covenants of Israel. The law did cast him out, but the grace of Jesus Christ will bring him in. Ishmael was cast out for Isaac's sake, but God will bring him into the Kingdom for Israel's sake.

When Israel sees the outstretched arm of God, the same that brought them out of Egypt, reach toward and bring Ishmael in from the wilderness and into the city of God, Israel will be provoked to jealousy for the Messiah. When God quenches the thirst of Ishmael in the waters of everlasting life, Israel will long for the water that once was hewn out of the rock.

The glory of God revealed to the Muslim people will anger Israel to seek the face of God. When Israel sees the Shekinah glory they rejected on the Mount manifested among the Muslim people, they will be angered and seek the face of God.

Imagine Ishmael saying to Israel:

- I was born of the bondwoman and *the law cast me out,* but the grace of Jesus Christ has brought me in.
- I was deprived of the *blessing of Abraham,* but now, in Christ Jesus, I am the seed of Abraham and an heir according to the promise (see Galatians 3:29).
- I grew up in the wilderness without a *father,* but now your God is my Father.
- I had no *inheritance* from my father, but now I have obtained an inheritance that you have not, because I am a son and *heir* of God through Christ.
- I have received the promise of the Holy Spirit as a deposit of my inheritance (see Ephesians 1:13-14).
- The new covenant I now walk in was promised to you by the prophets (see Jeremiah 31:33).
- I received the righteousness of God through faith without the law (see Romans 3:21-28).
- I have tasted and seen that the Lord is good (see Psalm 34:8).
- To you were committed the oracles of God, but unto me the Spirit of God (Romans 2:29).
- To you was the glory on the mount veiled in the face of Moses, but to me the exceeding glory is unveiled in the face of Jesus (see 2 Corinthians 3:7-9).
- To you was given the ministration of condemnation but unto me the ministration of righteousness (see 2 Corinthians 3:9).

Oh, how God uses the foolish things of this world to confound the wise (see 1 Cor. 1:27). The destiny of the Muslim people has long been hidden in Ishmael. God named him before birth, knowing one day he would be an instrument in the hand of God to provoke Israel to jealousy and anger.

Israel was in the wilderness for 40 years before entering the Promised Land, but Ishmael has been in the wilderness for 4,000 years, waiting to enter the promised land of God's salvation.

The Mystery of Israel's Sight

> *For I would not, brethren, that ye should be ignorant of this mystery, lest ye should be wise in your own conceits; that blindness in part is happened to Israel, until the fulness of the Gentiles be come in* (Romans 11:25).

Let us be careful not to be high-minded about our salvation and pointing fingers at the Jews for their stubbornness or their being cast away for a season. We are only partakers of the mercy of God. Let us not be wise in our own conceits and become ignorant of the mystery that blindness in part has happened to Israel, until the fullness of the Gentile population comes in.

God named him before birth, knowing he would provoke Israel to jealousy and anger.

Israel has been blinded by God for a season and only until the fullness of the Gentiles comes into the Kingdom. The rest of the world has been blinded by the god (satan) of this world (see 2 Cor. 4:4).

The fullness of the Gentiles must come in before the scales will fall off the eyes of Israel so they can see the Messiah. Nearly 42 percent of the world's Gentile population is Muslim. There can be no fullness of the Gentiles without the Muslim people. I believe the Muslim people are the epicenter for a Holy Ghost earthquake that will cause a tsunami of the glory of God to go into the nations of the world. They play a vital role in this end-time harvest.

When the world sees God the Father's outstretched arm to the Muslim people, the rest of the unbelieving world will long to know the Father. God is love; and whenever His love is displayed, the hungry human heart melts before Him. God will use Ishmael and the rest of the Gentiles to remove the scales from the eyes of the Jewish people.

When Israel recognizes the Messiah, they will seek after Him even in the midst of affliction (see Hos. 5:15). When their eyes are open, they will finally say, "*Blessed is He that cometh in the name of the Lord*" (Matt. 23:39). The return of the Lord is nigh.

"God Hears Me"

God named *Ishmael,* which means "God hears me," because one day He will hear the cry of the Muslim people and bring them into the Kingdom of God. It is also Ishmael's destiny to provoke the Church to a passion for Jesus Christ. The real key is—to bring Ishmael into the Kingdom of God for the sake of Israel.

Can you imagine Ishmael saying to the Jewish people, "I was deprived of the blessing of Abraham, but today I'm a seed in Christ of Abraham, and I have the blessing of Abraham"?

Imagine Ishmael saying:

"I was cast out of your father's house, and I was denied an inheritance. I was left in the wilderness to die, but today even though the law cast me out, the grace of Jesus Christ has caused me to come in."

Would those sayings provoke Israel? You better believe it! These truths coming from the lips of Ishmael who was long cast out, but who is returning, will provoke Israel. When Israel is provoked, they'll remember the words of Moses that were spoken to them.

> Provoking Israel to jealousy captures attention, provoking Israel to anger stirs passion.

Does God the Father want the Jewish people to know who the Messiah is? Does He still love them? Yes, and He has not forgotten about them. He has a plan for them; God desires to reach out to them. During this season of building one upon the other, God is reaching out to the Muslim people, and in His wisdom, He is preparing a stage for the nation of Israel and the Jewish people.

When they see the Shekinah glory manifest among the Muslim people, Israel will be angered and will seek the face of

God, because they will remember that glory and they will ask, "Why are these people seeing the glory that belongs to our God?" Then they will say, "We must seek His face."

Why would God want to provoke Israel? Because provoking gets our attention, and it will get their attention. When they are provoked to jealousy for their God, all their attention will go on their God and when all their attention goes on their God they're going to say one thing, "I need my Messiah." When they see others come to salvation, they will look to the Messiah for their salvation. They will realize that they need their Messiah and say, "We need our Messiah—we're the Messiah's people, where is the Messiah?"

Step One and Two

The first step to the Jewish salvation is for them to be provoked to jealousy. The second step for Jewish salvation is for them to be angered by seeing the glory of God, so they will seek the face of God. Hosea 5:15 says, even in the midst of tribulation and affliction they will seek the face of God. God wants to get their attention.

Romans 11:25 says, "For I would not, brethren, that you should be ignorant of this mystery, lest you should be wise in your own conceit." (In other words, get prideful.) "That blindness in part has happened to Israel until the fullness of Gentiles come in." So what is God saying? God is telling us through Paul who wrote the Book of Romans, that the Church should not get high-minded, prideful, or boastful—just because we received the salvation of Jesus and the Jewish people haven't...yet.

There is a mystery we don't understand about why "they have been blinded in part." What does He mean, blinded in part? A part of them did receive revelation to who Jesus is, and part did not. Obviously, some did or we wouldn't have the New Testament, because all of the writers are Jewish. So He's saying, part of them have been blinded. That's the mystery. God has blinded them for a season.

Although all of humankind has been blinded by the god of this world, He is talking about Israel and how even their hearts are blinded, along with their ability to spiritually see who the Messiah is—blinded until a certain time.

Hearts are blinded for a season.

This is evident throughout the Scriptures. The Book of Corinthians talks about every time they read the law of Moses there is a veil before them and they can't see, until their heart turns to the Lord. Their hearts are blinded. The enemy may work in the mind realm and blind the minds of people, but in this particular case, God has blinded the hearts of the Jewish people for a season, only for a season.

Until when? Until the fullness of the Gentiles comes in. This is the challenge: we can't get the fullness of Gentiles in without the Muslim people, because 42 percent of the Gentiles are Muslim. So if you attract all the other Gentiles on the planet to seek salvation, and you don't reach any Muslims, the fullness hasn't come in and Israel's eyes aren't opening. In the meantime, Israel is suffering.

God's Way

What is the way of God? The first shall be last and the last shall be first (Matt. 20:16). He separated Abraham, Isaac, and Jacob, and made them first. He made Israel first from the nations, from the Gentiles, but He's saying now that the first shall be last. Israel has become last and the Gentiles have become first, have they not?

But now we're moving into a time when God is looking over the earth and over the Muslim people. He's looking over the Gentiles; He's looking at the harvest fields, and they are ripe and ready for harvest. And He is also looking at the Jewish people, and He hears their cry, their affliction. He hears the cry of the people in the wilderness; He hears the cry of the people in the Church, and God the Father is saying, "It's the culmination of ages, it's the time to put everything back together. It's the time to reconcile things in Christ."

It's time...

It's a time for Him to move and that's why He is working on several levels and several realms around the globe. And this is the season of advancement for the Kingdom of God. That's what God is doing. But the fullness of Gentiles can't come in without the Muslim people coming in. Like Saul of Tarsus, I believe that the scales are about to fall off the eyes of Israel and the Jewish people, and they will recognize and see who the Messiah is.

Israel must:

- Be provoked to jealously.
- Be angered so they will seek the face of God.
- See the fullness of Gentiles come in so scales will be removed from their eyes.

Romans 11:26 says, "and so all Israel shall be saved." But, he says, right *after* the fullness of Gentiles comes in (see Rom. 11:25). So all Israel shall be saved, as it is written, "There shall come out of Zion the deliverer and shall turn away ungodliness from Jacob" (Rom. 11:26).

God has never forgotten about the Jewish people. The covenant that He promised them was the New Covenant that Jesus shed His blood for and that New Covenant is for them also. They have been blinded to it and don't see it and they're going to come into it. But before they can come and have the scales removed, God wants to get their attention, get their focus. Then He wants to get their heart; He wants to get their passion. When God provokes Israel to jealousy, He will get their attention. When He provokes them to anger, He will get their passion.

In order to get that passion and their focus, He will move mightily over the Gentile world—scales will fall from their eyes, and they will recognize and see who the Messiah really is.

In Matthew 23:37-39, Jesus is weeping over Jerusalem and says, "Oh Jerusalem, Jerusalem, you that killed the prophets and stoned them which are sent unto you. How often would I have gathered thy children together, even as a hen gathers her chicks under her wings and you would not! Behold your house is left unto you desolate. For I say unto you, you shall not see me henceforth till ye shall say, 'blessed is He that comes in the name of the Lord.'"

They will not recognize Him until they say, "Blessed is He that comes in the name of the Lord." This saying and this cry has to emerge from the Jewish people before they will see Him. First, they have to recognize Him before they can know His identity and cry out to Him. Being provoked to jealousy and then to anger will help them focus on the One who will cause the scales to be removed when the fullness of Gentiles comes in. Then they will know who the Messiah is, and they will say, "Blessed is He who comes in the name of the Lord!"

When that cry rises to Heaven, you know the Lord Jesus is coming back.

Religiously Stupid

The word *foolish* in Greek means "religiously stupid." I can't think of anything more religiously stupid than suicide bombers. Of course not all Muslim people are bombers, but you must understand that is the mindset we're dealing with.

Do you realize the seriousness of this situation—is it pricking your heart? God loves the Jewish people. He loves them so much that He's going to provoke them to jealousy, by reaching out and showing His goodness to Ishmael. Didn't God say "I'll have compassion on whom I'll have compassion, I'll show mercy to whom I'll show mercy"? (See Rom. 9:15.)

Who are we to get in the way of God? We need to have a right attitude about the Jewish people, the Church, and all Gentiles.

Then you will have no room to give offense but will help them realize Jesus as their personal Savior. That's what Jesus desires. Romans 11:15 says: "if the casting away of them [Jewish people] be the reconciling of the world, what shall the receiving of them be, but life from the dead?"

He says that even their casting away was a blessing to the Gentiles! Their stumbling was a blessing to us; we should be grateful; we should have more love for them. Rather than having a prideful heart, we should see the Jews as God's chosen people.

> *For if the first fruit be holy the whole lump is holy and if the root be holy so are the branches. And if some of the branches be broken off, and you being a wild olive tree were grafted in among them with them partakers of the root and with them partakers of the root and fatness of the olive tree. Boast not against the branches but if thou boast thou bearest not the root but the root thee* (Romans 11:16-18).

He is the root, and God started it all. Israel is the root; Abraham was root. God shall bless all the families of the earth, in one seed, which we know is Jesus. Israel who was first became last so that we could become first.

> *Thou wilt say then, The branches were broken off, that I might be grafted in. Well, because of unbelief they were broken off and if you stand by faith, be not high minded but fear. For if God spared not the natural branches, take heed lest He also spare not thee. Behold therefore the goodness and severity of God on them which fell, severity; but toward you goodness* (Romans 11:19-22).

God's severity toward the Jews ended up being your goodness. Meaning, their casting away or their stumbling being salvation for you, the Gentiles, coming into the Church. What is the Church? The Church is the third group that Paul was talking about. The Church is the born-again entity made up of Jew and Gentile alike. That is what it says in the Book of Ephesians and Colossians. Jew and Gentile alike, it doesn't matter if you're bond or slave, Jew or Gentile—we are all the Body of Christ, the Church.

The Church is Jew and Gentile alike.

For All of Us

Eve, Adam's wife, was bone of his bone and flesh of his flesh, but what about Jesus and us? We're not bone of His bone and flesh of His flesh. The Book of Ephesians says we are His bone and we are His flesh because we're one with Him. From the first Adam's side, God took and from one He made two. From the last Adam's side (Jesus), a hole was ripped while He was on the Cross, symbolizing that two would become one.

There is revelation in the Cross which is the key to everything. But the wisdom of God reveals the Cross. Did you know that Jesus was hanging on the Cross for six hours? Did you know that prior to being hung on the Cross they beat him, stripping his back, exposing his bones? They broke a reed on His head, bruised Him, punched Him, and then the third hour of the day they crucified Him (see Mark 15).

In the third hour of the day they pounded nails the size of nickels through His hands and feet and nailed Him to the Cross. From the 6th hour to the 9th hour, darkness covered the entire earth. Jesus was on the Cross for six hours because six is the number of man and that's who He was on the Cross for—all of us.

While He was on the Cross blood spilled from His body and spilled into the dirt from which humanity was made, symbolic of redemption. The Cross is not foolishness, but the wisdom of God.

Why did He have to wear a crown of thorns? So we could once again wear a crown of glory, because the first Adam fell short of the glory of God and lost his crown. Why were there holes in his hands? Because the hand is the covenant of friendship, and Jesus is a friend who sticks closer than a brother (see Prov. 18:24), and He is the Mediator between Heaven and earth, between humanity and God. Why were there holes put in his feet? So our feet would be shod with the preparation of the gospel of peace and that we can go into all the world (Eph. 6:15). There's wisdom in the Cross.

Jesus is coming again; this is an end-time message.

Meditation Moment

Hearing the terrorists chant to Allah while committing acts of violence would make most people doubt they would ever turn to Jesus as their Saviour. Only through the Holy Spirit can God's plan be interpreted so our finite minds can grasp it. How willing are we to consider an eternal blueprint drawn by the Creator Himself?

Chapter 5

Ishmael—The Next Forerunner

THERE'S another reason why God named Ishmael before birth by a divinely granted appearance of the angel of Lord, or God himself. There are only four people named this unique way. Two in the New Testament: John the Baptist and Jesus, and they are connected to the endtimes. The other two in the Old Testament: Ishmael and Isaac.

John the Baptist was first to be named before birth in the New Testament, and he was the forerunner for the Lord Jesus Christ. He was first because he was to serve the greater. He prepared the way in the power of the spirit of Elijah.

Likewise, Ishmael is the forerunner for the salvation of Isaac. That's why Ishmael was born first and Isaac second...because he was the forerunner. God is going to use Ishmael as a forerunner in our time.

Ishmael the forerunner.

God gave Abraham a dream in Genesis chapter 15. Deep sleep fell on Abraham. God told him that his descendents would end up in a strange land (meaning Egypt) and approximately 400 years later God would raise up a deliverer and bring them out. So was it God's plan to bring the children of Israel into Egypt?

Joseph was destined to end up in Egypt so he could be raised up to the right hand of Pharaoh and cause his family and the Israelites to be divinely situated in Egypt under the favor of a Pharaoh right into the path of prophecy. Let's look at the Scriptures.

> *So it came to pass, when Joseph had come to his brothers, that they stripped Joseph of his tunic, the tunic of many colors that was on him. Then they took him and cast him into a pit. And the pit was empty; there was no water in it. And they sat down to eat a meal. Then they lifted their eyes and looked, and there was a company of Ishmaelites, coming from Gilead with their camels, bearing spices, balm, and myrrh, on their way to carry them down to Egypt. So Judah said to his brothers, "What profit is there if we kill our brother and conceal his blood? Come and let us sell him to the Ishmaelites, and let not our hand be upon him, for he is our brother and our flesh." And his brothers listened. Then Midianite traders passed by; so the brothers pulled Joseph*

up and lifted him out of the pit, and sold him to the Ishmaelites for twenty shekels of silver. And they took Joseph to Egypt (Genesis 37:23-28 NKJV).

Joseph's brothers had a problem with the coat of many colors their father gave him. They were going to kill Joseph and tossed him into a dry, empty pit. What did God do about all of this? He sent a caravan of Ishmaelites by, and they bought Joseph and transacted him into the land of his destiny. His own brothers were going to thwart his destiny, but God in His Sovereignty sent Ishmael to prepare the way for Israel to be positioned into Eygpt through Joseph. When Israel is in trouble, God sends Ishmael.

When Israel is in trouble,
God sends Ishmael.

This was very pivotal to God's eternal purpose. He was positioning the Jewish people into Egypt so that he could eventually raise up the most powerful Pharaoh in the world and then show His power and might far above that pharaoh so that the whole world would know the power of the God of Israel. This was his desire and part of His plan that he revealed to Abraham (see Genesis 15:12-15).

The world thinks that God is trying to get them to fight each other, but no, God knows what He's doing. He uses Ishmael to help Israel. What about Moses the deliverer? Moses the deliverer went into the desert wilderness. He ended up with the Midianites, also known as Ishmaelites, which are the modern day Muslims in Iran (ancient Persia). He was trained with them so they kept him for a season until his time came to go to deliver Israel.

When Moses the deliverer was in trouble, God used the Ishmaelites. The Midianites and Ishmaelites are always referred to together, because the Midianites are part of the Ishmaelites. In that culture they worshiped the God of the first son, Ishmael. Ishmael has been a forerunner preparing the path for Isaac. Now is the time for Ishmael to be the forerunner for Isaac again. Ishmael was cast out for Isaac's sake but will be brought in as a forerunner for Israel's sake. Ishmael once again in these endtimes shall be a forerunner once again for Isaac.

God is preparing the way for Israel and Isaac to come into the Kingdom. That's why when Ishmael comes into the Kingdom, he shall be a voice crying in the wilderness. Just like God raised up John the Baptist to be a forerunner for Jesus, He's raising up Ishmael in this time to be a forerunner for Israel.

The Cup of Fury and Mercy

Have you heard people say that God is going to blow up everybody in the Middle East and all that kind of talk? There is a day of the Lord coming, and we know there's a time for judgment, a time for wrath. We understand that God didn't spare Sodom and Gomorrah, and He didn't spare the angels that sinned in Noah's time and so forth.

But let's not speed up His timing—there is a cup of fury that is filling up, and there's also a cup of mercy. The cup of fury is not full yet! And the wrath of the winepress will be poured out, but not yet. The cup of mercy has been overflowing for 2,000 years, and God desires that all men should be under mercy—the mercy of God.

Romans 11:30-31 says:

> *For as you in times past have not believed God, yet now have obtained mercy through their unbelief [the unbelief of the Jewish people] even so, have these also not believed that through your mercy they also may obtain mercy.*

It's all intertwined and connected with the great plan of God concerning the salvation of all peoples of the earth.

When God hears the cry of the Church, we're going to see Him. When God hears the cry of Ishmael, He's going to bring them into the Kingdom; but when He hears the cry of Israel the Lord Jesus Christ is going to return.

Revealing Himself

We're living in a time when the Father will reveal Himself.

On Friday, February 24, 1995, 7:30 in the morning while I was living in what I would call a basement of a basement, the Spirit of God suddenly came into my room. At the time, I thought the Holy Spirit only showed up in large crowds so I was a little surprised to find myself alone with him. I experienced a deep, mighty river flowing from the top of my head through to the bottom of my feet. It was pure love and the substance of Heaven, the very life of God. The Scriptures say a river flows from the throne of God and lamb above. (See Rev. 22:1.) This experience continued tangibly for three hours.

I heard an audible voice speak to me, words I never heard in all my life growing up as a Muslim. The voice of the Father said, *"I love you son, I love you son, I love you son."*

I could do nothing else but respond to him saying, "I love you Father, I love you Father, I love you Father."

I got up off the floor at 10:30 A.M. and noticed three things that had changed about me. First, I had an intense love for God like I never had before, and an intense hunger to know him more. Second, I had a much deeper, unconditional love for people. Third, I had an intense love for the Word of God. I picked up the Bible and could not put it down for 36 hours straight. As I looked at the page, it would explode inside my heart and understanding would flood my being. I supernaturally read the entire Bible in 36 hours.

> *...Man shall not live by bread alone, but by every word of God* (Luke 4:4; Deut. 8:3-4).

Fruit

I changed that day; and the fruit was evidenced in the fact that 99 percent of every person I knew—including Jews, Hindus, Sikhs, Muslims and atheists—gave their lives to Christ and were born again. It was truly by the Holy Spirit and by yielding to the river of reconciliation that approximately 1,500 people come to Christ. This happened only because of God and through my everyday living for Him, for this was long before I stepped out into full-time ministry. I was yielding to the river of reconciliation which should be the intention of every believer as it states in Second Corinthians 5:17-19.

Be committed to the word of reconciliation.

People began to accept Christ every day through the normal course of my everyday life. For example, I would lead "Joe" to Christ. After coming to Christ he would be excited and tell his friends and family. If they asked him questions he couldn't answer, he would meet me at the restaurant with the person with the question, and we would talk about Jesus. As mentioned previously, many people came to know the Lord during conversations at the restaurant.

My Deeper Revelation of the Father

When I came to Jesus it was a little hard for my Muslim mind to understand the concept of the Son of God. I knew He was the Son of God in my spirit, but my mind just didn't understand it. Jesus was always so gentle—He would walk me to the Father, and the Father would pour into me and love me. The Father would talk to me and show me His purposes, my destiny, and tell me how much He loved me.

Then the Father whispered in my ear, "Do you know why you can know me as Father? It's because of Jesus, my Son." Immediately that love was transported toward Jesus, and then I went to Jesus and understood what He did for me. I am so grateful and thankful for what He did for me—for all of us. Then Jesus would reveal the Father in a deeper way by the Spirit of God. This cycle of love continues from the Father to the Son and back through the Holy Spirit in us.

That is how you grow in your relationship and fellowship with God. There's a cry in my generation for the Father. Every problem in the earth, every lack in humanity, every lack of wholeness, Jesus is the answer, and His answer is the Father.

Matthew 11:27-28, "All things are delivered unto me of my Father and no man knows the Son but the Father, neither knows any man the Father save the son and he to whomsoever the son reveals the Father. Come unto me all ye that labor and are heavy laden, and I will give you rest."

What is the rest that Jesus gives? It's a revelation of His Father, because He's the only one who can give that rest. When He gives you greater revelation of the Father that's greater than your circumstance, then you will have peace and you will have the rest that only Jesus gives.

Jesus says, "Take My yoke upon you and learn of Me for I am meek and lowly in heart and you shall find rest unto your souls. For My yoke is easy and My burden is light" (Matt. 11:29-30). Would you consider what Jesus went through on earth as an easy yoke or a light burden? Most would say no—but Jesus had a greater revelation of the Father. That's why He said, except I see the Father do it, I don't do it, and except I hear the Father say it, I don't say it. I'm just here to please the Father I'm here to fulfill what's written of me in the volume of the Book.

Jesus came to please His Father.

Jesus was caught up with His Father—the Living Father sent Him so He lived by Him. (See John 6:57.) We must have a revelation of the Father to experience the rest that Jesus gives. So the Spirit of the Father reveals Jesus and the Spirit of His son reveals the Father.

Love

John the apostle was the only one of the original apostles of the Lamb who died a natural death—all of the others were martyred. There was definitely no shortage of people desiring to kill him. History tells us they tried to burn John in boiling oil, but for some reason they could not kill him. In fact, John was exiled, banished to the isle of Patmos where he wrote the Book Revelation.

Let me share an interesting scriptural fact. Through his writings in the Gospel of John he does not even mention his name. Instead he identifies himself as "the disciple whom the Lord loves." I would like to suggest that when he came up out of the boiling oil he probably said, "I'm the disciple whom the Lord loves—and you just can't kill love."

That's how Jesus is. He declared to the world the love of the Father. (See John 17:26.) Love will make you more than a conqueror. That's why they couldn't touch Him, and that's why on the Cross they couldn't kill Him until the Father separated from Him, then He died. When you know the Father, when you know Love, you can survive; you can overcome, because you are more than a conqueror.

Grace will get you through the problem. Faith will give you the victory. But love will make you more than a conqueror, and that is a state of being. It is not a temporary moment in your life that makes you who you are. It's not just something you've been through, it's something you become through the love that He loves you with. We are more than conquerors through Him who loves us. (See Romans 8:37.)

Grace for power. Faith for victory.

The times we are living in need people who are more than conquerors. We're going to need people who know the love that He loves them with—nothing will touch them. That's the kind of revelation Ishmael's going to have in the face of the enemy because when Ishmael is born of the Spirit of God, the archer will become an arrow in the bow of God's hand and will be shot into the heart of the enemy.

Ishmael has a cry for the Father, and he's going to know his Father, and Jesus is going to make it happen. Jesus is the one who will reveal the Father. That's why today Jesus has His own reputation in the Middle East and in the Muslim world. He is going ahead and fulfilling His Father's desire so they can know the Father, fulfill their destiny, and come into the Kingdom. God is going to manifest Himself worldwide through visions and dreams because there is destiny involved, and He's sovereignly doing something.

"Come Hither"

In Revelation chapter 1, John says:

I was in the Spirit on the Lord's day and heard behind me a great voice as of a trumpet, saying I am Alpha and Omega the first and the last. What you see write in the book and send it to seven Churches which are in Asia, Ephesus, Smyrna, unto Pergamus, Thyatira, unto Sardis, Philadelphia and Laodicea.

And I turned to see the voice that spake with me and being turned I saw seven golden candlesticks and in the midst of seven candlesticks are one like the Son of Man clothed with the garment down to the foot and gird about the paps with a golden girdle. And his head and hair was white like wool, as white as snow and His eyes were as a flame of fire and his feet like a fine brass as if they burned in a furnace and his voice as the sound of many waters.

And he had in his right hand seven stars and out of his mouth went a sharp two-edged sword and his countenance was as the sun shines in its full strength. When I saw him I fell at his feet as if dead and he laid his right hand upon me, saying unto me fear not I am the first and the last. I am he that lives and was dead and behold I am alive forevermore. Amen, he says amen. And have the keys of hell and death. Write the things which thou has seen and the things which are and the things which shall be hereafter (Revelation 1:10-19).

John was in the Spirit on the Lord's day, and suddenly he comes up to a higher level and sees Jesus in a dimension he's never seen him before. He has a revelation of Jesus he's never had before. Who gave him the revelation? The Father. Because he was in the Spirit on the Lord's day, the Spirit of the Father revealed Jesus to him in a greater dimension than ever before. Then while he's hanging out with Jesus, just like he heard the voice of the trumpet, look what happens:

> *After this I looked and behold a door was open in heaven and the first voice which I heard was as it were of a trumpet talking with me, which said, Come up hither and I will show thee things which must be hereafter. And immediately I was in the Spirit and behold a throne was set in Heaven and the one that sat on the throne* (Revelation 4:1-2).

The minute he had a revelation of Jesus, Jesus turned around and said let me give you a *greater* revelation of the Father. "Come up hither" to a higher place in the Spirit and see where He is sitting, the One on the throne. The Father wants to reveal His Son, and the Son by the Spirit wants to reveal the Father. This is the cycle that God wants us in as a Church, so we can be in Him, and He can be in us—so we can experience the life of God to its fullness.

I believe there is a door open in the spirit for you as a people to arise to a higher level, to go to a higher place. You are already in a good place; you are in the Spirit. But there is a higher place. Some things He will come and share with you right where you, are but other things He will not share with you until you come up to where He is. There are certain things He can only speak to you about when you come to where He is. He will show you things hereafter, but you must "come up hither."

> There is a higher place.

How did John reach that higher level? John fell dead when he first saw Jesus (Rev. 1:17). He was not at a height where he could withstand the glory of God in that capacity at that level and degree of revelation. Then Jesus touched him with His right hand, strengthened him, and expanded his capacity by the Spirit so he could stand up and withstand a greater measure of His glory. This is how God expands you; He needs to expand our capacity to withstand more of the glory of God. How does He do it? By revelation knowledge and by the touch of His hand.

May He grant you according to his riches and glory to be strengthened with all might by His Spirit in your inner most being. (See Ephesians 3:16.) The Spirit of God will strengthen you and infuse you with the glory of God, and your capacity will be increased to withstand more of the glory of His presence. If you can't withstand it how are you going to carry it?

We're supposed to be carriers and containers of the glory of God with the New Covenant is written on our hearts. Revelation paves the path for you to come up higher.

The Last Shall Be First and the First Last

Let's recap, the first man, Adam, was created. Generations later, in the time of Noah, the great, grand flush happened. After which Noah replenished the earth, and in doing so Noah gave birth to the nations—that's how the world's nations evolved. Then, eight generations later, God choose Abraham and separated him from the nations. (The word *nations* in the Bible is "Gentiles" or "goyim.")

Then God separated Isaac from Ishmael and Jacob from Esau. There is a pattern developing; obviously through Abraham, Isaac, and Jacob He separates Himself a people—the Jewish people, Israel.

During this early time in the earth's history there were only two major groups of people, the Jewish people and the Gentile people. The Jewish people had a covenant with God that started with Abraham, Isaac, and Jacob. Jacob, whose name became Israel, spawned 12 tribes which became a nation.

Romans 10:19 says,

> *but I say, Did not Israel know? First Moses said, I will provoke you to jealousy by them that are no people, and by a foolish nation I will anger you. But Isaiah is very bold and says, I was found of them that sought me not, I was made manifest unto them that asked not after me.*

Paul the apostle, who wrote the Book of Romans, had a heart for the Jewish people, the brethren of his flesh. He says that he aches for them, and wishes that he would be cursed that they might be saved (see Romans 10:1). Although he had a heart for the Jews, he was called as an apostle to the Gentiles. It was the heart of God in him for the Jewish people that caused him to have revelation from God and to speak mysteries to us concerning the Jewish people in Israel.

In chapter 10, Paul reminds them of something the prophet Moses said which is recorded in Deuteronomy 32:21. Notice that Deuteronomy chapters 31, 32, and 33 are the last words of the Lord that Moses gives to Israel as a people. He then pronounces a blessing, and he dies. He knew he was going home; and chapters 31 and 32 are valuable, final words that Moses, the prophet like none other, shared with the people of Israel.

Moses goes into history in Deuteronomy 32, and he talks about how they trusted in the rock that is perfect in all ways. Then he talks about how they rejected the rock, and their history, and he begins to deal with them a little bit.

> *But Jeshurun (Israel) waxed fat and kicked: thou art waxen fat, thou art grown thick, thou art covered with fatness. Then he forsook God which made him and lightly esteemed the rock of his Salvation. They provoked him to jealousy with strange gods, with abominations provoked they Him to anger. They sacrificed unto devils, not to God, to gods whom they knew not, to new gods that came newly up, whom your father's feared not.*
>
> *Of the Rock that begot them, thou are mindful of the rock that begot thee thou are unmindful and has forgotten God that formed you. And when the Lord saw it He abhorred them because of the provoking of his sons and his daughters.*
>
> *And He said, I will hide my face from them and I will see what their end shall be for they are a very forward generation of children in whom is no faith. They have moved me*

> *to jealousy with that which is not God. They have provoked me to anger with their vanities and I will move them to jealousy with those which are not a people, I will provoke them to anger with a foolish nation* (Deuteronomy 32:15-21).

Back to Romans chapter 10 where there is a key, a warning for Israel. "That a time will come, a time will come that God will provoke you to jealousy by them that are no people. And he says, by a foolish nation I will anger you. How will God provoke Israel to jealousy? Paul gives us insight in Romans 11:11 "by the Spirit of God I say then, have they [Jews] stumbled, that they should fall?" Paul ends with a question mark. Yes, they've stumbled but that doesn't mean they've fallen, that means they're not completely done with or out of the picture. But rather, through their fall salvation has come unto the Gentiles to provoke them to jealousy. So what provokes Israel to jealousy? The salvation of the Gentiles.

That's God's goodness; our God is a good God. In the eyes of the New Covenant, He expresses His goodness in every way. His way to express His goodness is to show salvation to the Gentile people, and no one can argue with His generosity. In doing so, He actually provokes the Jewish people unto jealousy.

God is a good God.

There's no greater "Gentile" that God could reach out to provoke Israel to jealousy than the Muslim people. Ishmael was the one from whom God separated Isaac, but Ishmael was actually cast out for Isaac's sake. Ishmael was cast out from Abraham's house, left without a father in the wilderness to die. The Jewish people are greatly thankful and take great pride in the fact that God separated Abraham from the nations, Isaac from Ishmael and Jacob from Esau.

Consequently, the one people group that Israel would not like God to reach out to are the people who surround them geographically right now—Muslim nations. Israel is surrounded by the Muslim world—their enemy.

God has a plan.

Meditation Moment

God's ways are not our ways. His plans are the only ones that lead to His Kingdom come. Have there been times when you thought you had a situation under control only to find that your plan stranded you in totally unfamiliar circumstances? God's plan for Israel and Ishmael may seem unfamiliar to us but our hearts yielded to Him will reveal the truth.

Chapter 6

Terrorism and Islam

The Spirit of Esau

THERE is an element of terrorism and war within the Muslim world today. This particular element is at the center of the world's stage. With all the television and media coverage, it is a difficult subject to ignore. Some countries are concerned about the rapid growth of Muslim populations within their borders, for fear of potential Islamic fundamentalism. Dormant cells of fundamentalists are scattered across the Western world, leaving much concern for a new enemy from within.

Governments today face the problem of identifying potential terrorists because they live simple lives and carry on business as usual—until suddenly one day they answer the call to holy war.

Because governments do not want to point fingers at the Muslim world at large and cause unnecessary upheaval, they face a dilemma—*how do they keep their population safe while at the same time seek out those who wish to harm citizens?* There are many unanswered questions about the origins and extent of terrorism and violence in the Muslim world.

This chapter shares with you biblical insights about Esau, then Ishmael and Esau, and their connection to terrorism.

Rebekah, Isaac's wife, was the mother of Esau and Jacob. She was pregnant with twins, and even before birth, these two nations struggled with one another in her womb. She went to ask the Lord about all this:

> *And the children struggled together within her; and she said, If it be so, why am I thus? And she went to inquire of the Lord. And the Lord said unto her, Two nations are in thy womb, and two manner of people shall be separated from thy bowels; and the one people shall be stronger than the other people; and the elder shall serve the younger* (Genesis 25:22-23).

Esau was to serve the younger, though contrary to normal tradition and culture. Two very differently natured people were separated from her womb, and Esau became stronger than Jacob. Today, the people of Esau are stronger than the people of Jacob.

> *And the boys grew: and Esau was a cunning hunter, a man of the field; and Jacob was a plain man, dwelling in tents* (Genesis 25:27).

Esau grew up a skilled hunter; he was a man of the wild. Esau was a strong man; his descendants would be much like him.

Esau's Birthright and Jacob's Blessing

Esau sold his birthright for a bowl of soup. He came in tired from the field and begged Jacob for some "red pottage" (see Genesis 25:30). Esau despised his birthright and sold it for a bowl of lentils and bread (see Genesis 25:31-34).

Isaac was getting old, and his eyes were dim. He wanted to pass on the blessing of Abraham to his eldest son, Esau, before he died. So Isaac sent him out to hunt some game and prepare food for him so he could eat it and bless Esau:

> *Now therefore, please take your weapons, your quiver and your bow, and go out to the field and hunt game for me. And make me savory food, such as I love, and bring it to me that I may eat, that my soul may bless you before I die* (Genesis 27:3-4 NKJV).

Rebekah overheard Isaac and told Jacob to fetch some meat, so that she could make the food for Isaac, in order that Jacob could receive the blessing from Isaac instead of Esau. She devised a plan to dress Jacob with Esau's clothes so that he would smell like Esau. She also covered his arms and neck with goat hair so that Jacob would seem as hairy as Esau (see Genesis 27:14,17). The plan worked, and Isaac blessed Jacob and gave him the blessing of Abraham. Isaac blessed Jacob, and the blessing is recorded in two parts in the Bible:

Therefore God give thee of the dew of heaven, and the fatness of the earth, and plenty of corn and wine: Let people serve thee, and nations bow down to thee: be lord over thy brethren, and let thy mother's sons bow down to thee: cursed be every one that curseth thee, and blessed be he that blesseth thee (Genesis 27:28-29).

And God Almighty bless thee, and make thee fruitful, and multiply thee, that thou mayest be a multitude of people; And give thee the blessing of Abraham, to thee, and to thy seed with thee; that thou mayest inherit the land wherein thou art a stranger, which God gave unto Abraham (Genesis 28:3-4).

Esau came home with his hunted game and cooked a meal for his father, Isaac; only to find out that Jacob had already received the blessing. Esau wept and begged Isaac for any additional blessing for himself. Isaac could not give him the blessing of Abraham or the blessing of the firstborn, but Isaac answered Esau:

And by thy sword shalt thou live, and shalt serve thy brother; and it shall come to pass when thou shalt have the dominion, that thou shalt break his yoke from off thy neck (Genesis 27:40).

Esau hated Jacob because of the blessing that Isaac blessed Jacob with. Esau sold his birthright to Jacob and also lost the blessing of his birthright. Esau now planned in his heart to kill Jacob (see Genesis 27:41).

Esau sold his birthright and lost the blessing.

Jacob became Israel. Even today, Esau hates Israel. Esau does live by the sword, and Esau's descendents are a people stronger than Israel. Esau has always been at war with Jacob. The struggle that began in their mother's womb continues. Jacob grabbed hold of Esau's heel when he was born, and ever since, Esau has believed he will crush Jacob under his heel.

Esau Marries into Ishmael's Lineage

Esau went to Ishmael, his uncle, and married his daughter, Mahalath. Ever since then, Esau and Ishmael have been mingled together in covenant.

> *Then went Esau unto Ishmael, and took...Mahalath the daughter of Ishmael Abraham's son, the sister of Nebajoth, to be his wife* (Genesis 28:9).

Esau had other wives, but his marriage with Mahalath is the one that forged an alliance between Esau and Ishmael, which still exists today. Esau went to his uncle, Ishmael, with hatred in his heart for Jacob. Ever since Esau married Ishmael's daughter, the seed of Esau has been mingled with the descendents of Ishmael.

Today, mingled with Ishmael, is Esau, who has always been at war with Jacob (Israel). Ishmael was spoken of as being a man of war, and Esau was destined to live by the sword. They both were archers but with different intentions. Ishmael was an archer for survival in the wilderness war. Esau was a hunter of the wild, more interested in hunting his prey and celebrating his strength over Jacob, the worker of the fields. Esau lived by the sword, and Ishmael was always at war.

Man divides; God separates unto Himself.

My intent is not to focus on the literal blood descendents of Esau, for God loves the descendents of Esau the same as all people on the face of the earth. However we must gain insight into the spirit or nature of Esau to understand why God is exposing the face of terrorism in Islam today.

The Spirit of Esau—the Crisis of Islam

Islam is in a modern-day crisis. What brought Esau and Ishmael together is now bringing a separation in Islam. The cry of Ishmael and the pain of Esau that once united them are now forces that divide them. God is exposing the spirit of Esau in the face of terrorism. Terrorism and Islam have become synonymous in the world today. Actually, the spirit of Esau is the spirit of terrorism in Islam.

There are two groups of people among Islam today, those who have the cry of Ishmael in their hearts and those who have the intent of Esau in their hearts. I'm not talking about Sunni or Shiias, I'm talking about the two types of hearts among the Muslim people. One group is the majority of Muslims, with the cry of Ishmael in their hearts. This cry is the longing to be accepted and loved by a father, to have an inheritance, to find blessing from the father, and to find approval and an inheritance. This is the heart and the cry of the majority of the Muslim people today. They see terrorism and realize that Islam has not answered the cry of their own hearts. They are still hungry and thirsty in a spiritual wilderness, looking for God to respond to the crisis in Islam.

Ishmael's cry and Esau's pain
that once united, now divides.

The other group is comprised of Muslims who have embraced the spirit of Esau and have sold their natural birthright to terrorism, with no regard for life. They are willing to strap a bomb around their chest and die in the hope of waking up in paradise with 72 virgins. This spirit is not interested in peace, but in terrorism until death. This spirit has been around for generations. This group includes the terrorists and those who favor them. Thankfully this group is the minority.

To gain deeper insight into terrorism, we need to know more about Esau. At the heart of this spirit is hatred for Israel, because of the blessing Isaac blessed Jacob with instead of Esau. Esau became the father of Edom and the Edomites. Islam came through Ishmael's son Kedar, ancestor of the prophet of Islam, to the great nation of Ishmael and to the nation of Esau.

Genesis 36:1 says, "Now these are the generations of Esau who is Edom." There are two things about Edom to notice: 1. Edom is a *people* because that is who Esau is and his descendants. 2. Edom is also a *place,* a land where Esau dwelt. Today the land of Edom is in southern Jordan—beneath the tip of Israel. This is the land and the people we're talking about.

There is scriptural proof that this attitude or spirit of war continued on in their descendants even though Jacob and Esau made peace with each other. For example Psalm 137:7 (AMP) says: "Remember, O Lord, against the Edomites, that they said in the day of Jerusalem's fall. Down, down to the ground with her!" When Babylon came in and took over Jerusalem the Scripture records that the Edomites, or the descendants of Esau, helped Babylon, and they went in and took all the spoils of Jerusalem and took advantage of Jacob and all his children and the Israelites.

There has always been a problem—that's why prophetically in the Scripture the prophecy about Edom is very serious. It is very negative in terms of the prophetic things spoken about Esau and the descendants of Esau in the Bible.

Ishmael's descendents embraced Islam, looking for the answer to the cry of their hearts, and the descendents of Esau embraced Islam as the means of expression of his heart. Today, the spirit of Esau is expressing itself through the face of terrorism in Islam. The heart or spirit of Esau is among Ishmael today. This spirit hates Jacob (Israel) and wants to kill him.

The cry of the Muslim people goes back 4,000 years to the heart of Ishmael, long before Islam. This cry is still roaring in the hearts of Muslims around the world today. While terrorism is being unveiled in the face of Islam, the Muslim people find their cries unanswered.

The Prophets Speak

And saviours shall come up on mount Zion to judge the mount of Esau; and the kingdom shall be the Lord's (Obadiah 1:21).

The entire Book of Obadiah is a vision the prophet had about the present, past, and future of Esau and his descendents. Esau and his descendents rejoiced at the destruction and captivity of Israel much like the modern-day terrorists celebrate the destruction of their enemies. Notice the word *saviours* in verse 21, speaking of believers in Jesus the Messiah.

For thy violence against they brother Jacob shame shall cover thee, and thou shalt be cut off for ever. In the day that thou stoodest on the other side, in the day that the strangers carried away captive his forces, and foreigners entered into his gates, and cast lots upon Jerusalem, even thou wast as one of them. But thou shouldest not have looked on the day of thy brother in the day that he became a stranger; neither shouldest thou have rejoiced over the children of Judah in the day of their destruction, neither shouldest thou have spoken proudly in the day of distress. You shouldest not have entered into the gate of my people in the day of their calamity; yea, thou shouldest not have looked on their affliction in the day of their calamity. Nor have laid hands on their substance in the day of their calamity (Obadiah 1:10-13).

This is further evidence that the descendants of Esau have continued to war against Jacob. The hatred remains. The hatred that began in Esau's heart continues today among a small, fundamental militant group of Muslims, and that is the spirit that is driving them. We war not against flesh and blood, but against the spirit realm. That is the spirit that is driving them and trying to camouflage the destiny of the Muslim people.

Why is this an important key to understanding terrorism? The Scripture says in Amos 1:11, "Thus saith the Lord, For three transgressions of Edom, and for four, I will not turn away the punishment thereof, because he did pursue his brother with the sword, and did cast off all pity, and his anger did tear perpetually, and he kept his wrath for ever."

Peace did not last—hatred continued on among descendants and the generations of Esau, and it has been mingled among the Muslim people.

The Bible: Cure for Terrorism

> *For we wrestle not against flesh and blood, but against principalities, against powers, against the rulers of the darkness of this world, against spiritual wickedness in high places* (Ephesians 6:12).

I learned a long time ago that the plans of the Spirit are birthed into this realm through prayer. God's Word is forever settled in Heaven but must be established on earth. We, as a people, must pray out the plan of God to be established on the earth. We must take authority over the spirit of Esau through prayer. When we pray, God exposes the deceitful strategies of the enemy and makes a way for His purposes to be established. Just as watchmen watch a city, so in the Kingdom, watchmen watch and pray in the Spirit against all principalities and powers, and can see what the enemy is trying to do and intercede for those in danger.

There are many Esau hearts who have sold their birthrights in this hour. Jacob came out of his mother's womb holding the heel of Esau. Ever since then, Esau has desired to crush Jacob under his heel, but the God of Jacob (Israel) will crush the spirit of Esau.

According to the Book of Hebrews, we have come unto mount Zion; the city of the living God, heavenly Jerusalem, and unto a Kingdom that cannot be shaken. These saviours on "mount Zion" are believers who understand the authority of the Kingdom they represent on earth. They recognize the kingdoms of this world shall become the Kingdoms of the Most High God. *The mount of Esau* represents the government of Esau, which is the spirit of Esau or spirit of terrorism in Islam today.

Ishmael saved, Esau judged.

Believers must pray and intercede from their seated position of authority in Christ, making way for the government of God to crush the spirit of Esau in this hour.

And the God of peace shall bruise satan under your feet shortly... (Romans 16:20).

The spirit of Esau hopes to camouflage the identity of Ishmael and abort his destiny. Simultaneously, this spirit of terrorism seeks to paralyze the Church with a fear of reaching out to Muslims. This spirit holds many people hostage and is abusing the hidden treasure of Ishmael.

Many focus on Esau, while God waits to hear the cry of Ishmael so He may show the Muslim people the face of Jesus Christ.

> *For thus hath the Lord said unto me, Within a year, according to the years of an hireling, and all the glory of Kedar shall fail: And the residue of the number of archers, the mighty men of the children of Kedar, shall be diminished: for the Lord God of Israel hath spoken it* (Isaiah 21:16-17).

Kedar was the second son of Ishmael, ancestor to Muhammad, the prophet of Islam. These archers and mighty men seem to carry the description of the modern-day terrorist. The nature of the spirit of Esau is that of a hunter and archer who seeks out his prey and attacks with no value for life. Esau kept his wrath forever against Jacob and the symbol of his wrath was always the sword aimed at Israel.

> The spirit of Esau
> is the spirit of terrorism in Islam today.

> *Thus saith the Lord; For three transgressions of Edom, and for four, I will not turn away the punishment thereof;*

because he did pursue his brother with the sword, and did cast off all pity, and his anger did tear perpetually, and he kept his wrath for ever (Amos 1:11).

The controversial element of the sword among the Muslim people is courtesy of the spirit of Esau. This spirit has camouflaged the destiny of Muslim people, making us deaf and blind to the cry and face of Ishmael. God, with one hand, is reaching out to Ishmael and, with the other hand, is judging the spirit of Esau. The spirit of Esau is looking for new followers; and an entire generation of Muslims lies in the valley of decision, frustrated with a cry unanswered.

Terrorism is becoming everyday news. Muslim terrorists raid Christian homes in Palestine; violence in Australia; destruction of hundreds of vehicles in France by frustrated and angry youth; and decades of random violence against Jews. Since 9-11-2001 there has been a lot of focus on terrorism. There are a lot of questions in the hearts of believers and the Church—what should we do about terrorism? What is it all about? What is the root of it, and where is it coming from? How do we respond and handle it?

First of all, we have to get God's perspective. We've got to hear what God says, not what the media says, not what television reporters say and newspapers print. At the end of the day if you don't know God's perspective about it, what are you going to base your decisions on? We must know what the Spirit of the Lord is saying, and what is in His Word when we get into times like this.

There is a crisis in Islam—and the crisis is terrorism. The face of terrorism is being exposed as Islam for a reason. God is allowing the face of terrorism to be exposed so that the world can look at it and the Muslim people can look at it and ask if this is the Islam they embraced—is it really what they want?

Jesus is the Answer.

Satan's Strategies

We need to shed some light on satan's strategies. First he desires to recruit a generation of young people disillusioned in the valley of decision while Islam is in the midst of a reformation.

Today, an entire generation is asking questions about terrorism, and they don't have the Answer. It is time we provide them with the Answer. Before the spirit of terrorism enlists new recruits, we need to share the gospel with them.

Why would they be attracted to terrorists and their plans of destruction? Why would it be attractive to a young generation? Genesis 27:42 says, "Behold, thy brother Esau, as touching thee, doth comfort himself, purposing to kill thee." There was a *comfort* that Esau was finding in wanting to kill his brother. That, of course, is a pseudo-comfort that the spirit of terrorism provides—an antidote to the disillusionment among Muslim young people.

These young people think they have been offered Heaven, and there's a comfort that goes along with this because they believe that they're doing God a service. They believe they are performing a holy act. They believe they are dying for the sake of Islam and the cause. They want to obtain eternity—and they don't want to miss it.

This is an attraction for young people and a major problem for the Christian and Jew. Remember, the average age of the Muslim population is around 30, and it is a picking field for the enemy.

Also, satan is trying to make the Church deaf to the cry of Ishmael and camouflage the destiny of Ishmael. God wants to awaken the Church to the cry of Ishmael's heart so that the Church can pray and intercede and lift up Ishmael to God so that cry can be awakened and heard by God.

So that is our dilemma today—how best to defeat the enemy's strategy. Whenever God has a destiny or plan for a people, a nation, or a group, the enemy always has a strategy to counteract, thwart, or delay it. He can't really stop it, but he can hinder it. I believe that is what is going on right now in the earth with terrorism—it's the enemy strategy to divert more people away from the saving grace of Christ.

The Church has to pray about these things to be uncovered so the Muslim people's destiny will be uncovered and will no longer remain camouflaged, that the cry would be awakened.

The destiny of Muslims has been camouflaged, making us deaf to the cry of Ishmael.

When God began to deal with me about terrorism, He said the demise of terrorism shall be "that the day will come when the terrorists will begin to kill their own people." He said it would be just like the way Hitler's demise came because he didn't care about his own people and they were slaughtered in the process of his world war. The same is true with Saddam Hussein. He didn't care for his own people, and his own people starved and died.

God says there will be a time when terrorists will kill Muslims. They will blow up Mosques, and although people say that's not possible, it will happen. Why? Because they are driven by a spirit, a spirit that knows no end. That's the thing about the devil, when he is exposed he begins to lose control, and he can't stop himself. The spirit of terrorism will increase before it comes to its demise. It will be diminished, but first it will increase.

Prayer

Zechariah 1:14-15 says:

so the angel that communed with me said unto me, Cry thou, saying. Thus saith the LORD of hosts; I am jealous for Jerusalem and for Zion with a great jealousy. And I am very sore displeased with the heathen that are at ease; for I was but a little displeased, and they helped forward the affliction.

Zachariah was a prophet who had eight visions, seemingly all at one time. He tells us that the nation of Israel, for example, missed out on the visitation of Jesus. They turned their back on God, they went after idols and so forth, and they got into a place of affliction. But then he says some people came along and helped forward that affliction because of the hatred in their heart. I believe he is referring to Esau and Edom and the spirit of terrorism. And that is what's happening today.

The world continuously asks, "What's going to happen next? All these terrorists are doing all these things in Jerusalem and Israel...is God going to come and judge them and punish them and blow them up? What's going to happen?"

Before that final Day of Judgment comes, there are things that will occur in stages. One includes the mercy of God reaching out, preserving, and bringing the people out of bondage who have the cry of Ishmael and are being held captive by the spirit of Esau. The spirit of Esau's intent is to express this spirit of terrorism and violence and gain attention.

We must pray against that spirit, and in the meantime we have to bring the people who have the cry of Ishmael in their heart, into salvation. We've got to let the cup of mercy reach out to them before things escalate, and we get closer toward the midnight hour of the endtimes. At the same time we must remember the two cups—a cup of fury which is about to overflow and the cup of mercy that has been overflowing for the past two thousand years while God is working His plan.

Endtimes

I would highly recommend reading and studying the entire Book of Obadiah—it paints the entire picture about what is and will happen. As mentioned previously, verse 21 says, "And saviours shall come up on mount Zion to judge the mount of Esau; and the kingdom shall be the Lord's." A mount represents government and kingdom authority in a way. Obadiah is talking about the domain and the government of the mount of Esau.

Now this could also have a physical implication of the actual coming of the Lord when He comes with all His saints. That could be the final annihilation. There's much to see unfold in the Book of Obadiah. I believe things are not going to be totally destroyed until the final coming day of the Lord, and that will be the time of judgment. But until then it can be held back and dealt with by the Church who has authority.

The Church must take authority by recognizing its seated position of authority in Christ, and through prayer and intercession take more ground while holding satan back to bring the people in. In other words, we the Church stand in the gap for these people.

We need to see God's heart for the Muslim people, but we also need to see the enemy exposed. When the enemy is exposed by His light, half the battle is already won because now the enemy does not have an advantage—we can see him. Tragedies like 9-11 won't surprise us anymore because we will be out there doing something to prevent them. We can't sit and watch TV and say, "Oh gee, what are we going to do? Oh Lord what are we going to do?" No, we're going to get involved and do our part. We're the Church; we're going to take authority. We're going to get involved.

We will deal with the spirit of terrorism, which we know now is the spirit of Esau, and we're going to get a hold of it so Muslim people can come into the Kingdom of God. The spirit of Esau is holding them hostage and keeping them from coming to salvation. That is the spirit you need to tackle ***in the Spirit*** by taking authority and declaring and decreeing the Word of the Lord and the direction He gives you.

Whenever you pray for Muslim people, the Holy Spirit will lead you to effectively pray for the cry of Ishmael. The Church needs to take authority, to do our part to get all people to come to Jesus. When we do, even terrorists will come to Jesus.

When I was in Nigeria preaching to pastors, someone testified who said he was a terrorist. After he got saved, they killed his wife and tried to kill him. Later, he led the terrorist to the Lord who killed his wife and left him for dead. He is now a born-again evangelist. That's pretty serious business, wouldn't you say?

Only the love of Jesus can produce those kinds of miracles. It's hard to swallow, but I know it's true. Don't underestimate God and what He's trying to do.

The enemy introduces terrorism because it is the season for the Muslims to come into the Kingdom. Terrorism causes the world and the Churches to say, "Forget the Muslim people, give up on them, let's get rid of them!" But God wants the Church to wake up and know that He has not forgotten them nor forsaken them, but He has a plan for them. And He wants to get the Church involved in His plan.

The enemy not only wants to rob Ishmael of his destiny, he also wants to rob him of his resources. According to the Institute for the Analysis of Global Security, the Middle East has 64 percent of the world's oil reserves.[1] Financial resources in part of that region are going toward funding terrorism.

God blessed Ishmael. But this is another way in which the enemy is trying to rob and thwart Ishmael's destiny and the destiny of the Muslim people. Our prayers need to focus on this key area as well because the enemy can't succeed if he doesn't have the funds to supply the terrorists.

God's Plan

God's plan will expose terrorism for what it is, and it shall fall and crumble—but first it will increase. Nations are allowing Muslims to enter as a way of trying to appease them—trying to divert terrorism attacks. But the fundamental radical Muslims take advantage of the liberties within free nations which causes even more concern.

How can we protect our cities from terrorism? You, the Church, are the light, you are the lighthouse in the city. (See Matt. 5:14-16). Terrorism is serious—for every country.

When I began to talk about this on our television program in Canada, I received an email from a well-known minister who had a vision. In the vision he saw a Christian down on the ground, and Muslims were beating him. The Lord spoke to the pastor and said this persecution will come to this nation if we don't follow in the ways of the Lord. Apparently, the Muslims will be used in this way.

The United States, Canada, England, have a destiny in Christ like other nations. Muslims have made a decision take over free nations, and they are diligently working on their goal. Once a nation becomes a Muslim nation, if it ever tries to convert back, the Muslims believe that they have the right to declare a holy war, a Jihad against infidels.

We know that God has a plan, but we should also realize the seriousness of these matters the world is facing. We've got to be balanced—not fearful, but aware of what's going on. Attune your spiritual radar. We need to allow righteousness back in our lands, and the churched need to be strategically involved in changing the course in our nations. There is but a short window of opportunity to affect change.

Balance terrorism with prophetic hope.

I believe that there is a remnant who will arise and hear the Word of the Lord. There is a remnant who will know what is of God and who will do exploits in His name. There is a remnant who will come to positions of leadership, come into places of authority, and will fulfill the destiny that is set before them. You will wonder, and you will marvel and ask where they come from. They were nobodies. They were obscure people; they were people of no importance. But God will raise them up and put them in places of authority. They will strategically do things that will help change the course of the nation and bring it into its destiny, to God's plan.

Strategies of Terrorism

Let me share with you seven strategies of terrorism in our day.

1. To camouflage the destiny of the Muslim people in the endtimes. Satan desires the Church to become blind to the plans and purposes of God for the Muslim world.

Terrorism is a smokescreen to distract the Church from its task. Terrorism is a reality, and there must be a precise balance between its threat and the hope that comes from the voice of the Holy Spirit in our times.

2. To make the world deaf to the cry of Ishmael in a season when God desires to awaken it and answer it.

3. To paralyze out of fear and divert God's love. Satan wants to paralyze the Church with fear so it will not reach out to the 1.6 billion Muslims who live around the world. Fear has a voice, and its language is lies and twisted versions of the truth. Faith works by love, but unbelief works by fear. When love speaks, faith listens; but when fear speaks, unbelief listens. Love speaks truth, and fear speaks lies. We actually forward the agenda of terrorism when we only speak of the evil and impending doom through the news, church pulpits, and other forms of communication.

4. To steal the natural and financial resources that are rightfully Ishmael's as a result of the blessing that God blessed him with. They have been stored up in the endtimes to fund the gospel. Keeping Ishmael poor in material goods as well as spiritually and mentally will maintain the indecisiveness that satan desires.

5. To recruit a generation of disillusioned youth and provide a deceptive, pseudo-comfort through the violence and death this spirit of Esau offers.

6. To rob Ishmael of his spiritual inheritance reserved through grace in Christ. Esau was a profane person

and lost his birth right to his inheritance and failed the grace of God through bitterness. This Esau spirit longs to see the same for Ishmael while desiring to kill Jacob. (See Hebrews 12:15-17.)

7. To infuse North America and the rest of the Western world with hopelessness. Scripture says hope deferred makes the heart sick, but a longing fulfilled is like tree of life. (See Prov. 13:12.) When hope is robbed ,our faith has no purpose, and our love has no remaining effect.

There is a great need to balance the evil intentions of terrorism and the prophetic hope inspired through the Scriptures concerning the salvation of the Muslim people. Theses terrorists desire to sow terror into the heart of America and paralyze the Church with fear. They are motivated by an unseen spiritual force, and have a faith fueled by the deceptive lies of the spirit of Esau. The more we hear the one-sided story of the terrorists, the more we miss out on the heartbeat of God for Muslims and refuse to participate and co-labor with Him. We must look past the natural and realize our war is with principalities, powers, rulers of darkness of this world and spiritual wickedness in high places

Perfect loves casts out all fear. While the enemy is trying to harden the heart of the Church with hatred for Muslims, Jesus is releasing His love into our hearts to tenderize us to hear the Word of the Lord for this season concerning *all* of God's children.

Meditation Moment

The majority of Muslims are not controlled by the violent spirit of Esau. Satan would have us believe that all Muslims want to harm us. Are you afraid of Muslims? Allowing the Holy Spirit to use us to reach out to Muslims will take obedience and confidence—in Him who has a plan to bring all into His Kingdom.

Endnote

1. http://www.iags.org/futureofoil.html.

Chapter 7

Reunion of Ishmael and Isaac

Revelation of the Father

OUR loving, heavenly Father heard the voice of Ishmael when he was left under a bush in the wilderness. God opened the eyes of his mother, Hagar, to a well of water from which he could drink and live. We are now living in a time when again Ishmael is crying out to God. God will hear his cry and open his eyes and show him the well of everlasting life, Jesus Christ.

The Church must pray that God will create a cry in the heart of the Muslim people so deep that it touches the heart of the Most High. We, the Church of God, must intercede for Ishmael like a mother would for a dying child. For God uses the Church to birth the plans of the Spirit into this realm through prayer.

Today, when God hears the cry of Ishmael, He will use the Church to give him water from the well of everlasting life. It took water to save his life from death in the wilderness. Today it will take living water to save him from death unto life eternal. God is going to use the conversion of Ishmael to stir up the Church, as God used the conversion of Saul to stir up the early Church in the midst of persecution.

The Lamb of God was slain before the foundation of the world, but manifested on Earth in the fullness of time.

God will use Ishmael to provoke the Church unto a passion for Jesus—what the Church has forsaken, Ishmael will embrace. God is going to use Ishmael to provoke Israel to jealousy for the Messiah. Thus far, you have read about what is going to happen, why it is significant to the times we are living in, and whom it will affect. Now I will share with you how all this will evolve.

Seasons and Times

The plan of God works in its season. For example, the Lamb of God was slain before the foundation of the world, but only manifested on earth in the fullness of time or the appointed season. The plan of God is forever settled in Heaven, but there is a season for it to be established on earth. God moves in appointed seasons of time. It is one thing to know what God is saying; it is another to discern the season He is speaking about.

A *kairos* moment opens the door to destiny, and that which has been hidden for ages is revealed. When time and eternity come together, the season of fulfillment and the Word of the Lord meet. Once the season is unveiled, and the Word is revealed, all that is left to do is respond. This *kairos* moment has already begun throughout the Muslim world.

Ishmael and Isaac

After being cast out of Abraham's house, the last time Ishmael saw his father was to bury him. And that was the last time that Ishmael and Isaac came together. Ever since that time they have been separated—until now. It was the *death* of a father that separated them. Now it will be the *revelation* of the Father that will bring them back together again—and there will be a family reunion in Christ Jesus.

You see, God loves *all* people; He's not a respecter of persons. We have to keep our perspective right, about the Jewish people and the Muslims. Now here's what I have experienced. Some people say that they love the Jewish people, but they don't like Ishmael. But they don't understand that Ishmael is the forerunner for Isaac!

We can't love Israel if we can't support Ishmael. We must have the heart of God because we need to be praying to help Israel reach its destiny. If you care about their salvation, you will care about having their eyes opened by seeing Gentiles saved—being provoked to jealousy to see the Messiah. Then they will rejoice in the joy of the Lord that they had to give up because they were first, but now became last.

Ishmael's mother was Egyptian. Ishmael married an Egyptian. And Egypt is a Muslim nation today. When Ishmael is converted there's going to be a mass movement in the land of Egypt. The land of Egypt is going to be used in a powerful way concerning the salvation of the Muslim people. God has not forgotten about that land, and there will be a movement of God throughout that region. There will be a move of God in Iran and Turkey, and many of the Middle Eastern countries are going to experience a move of God. You will see a harvest of Muslims coming into the Kingdom.

There is also a move of God coming to Europe. Right now Europe is very spiritually sensitive. It is a key strategic time, and we've got to get the gospel into Europe. I'm so grateful that God will tell us what's going on so we know as a Church know what to do—our God is awesome.

It's the revelation of the Father that will bring Ishmael and Isaac back together again. When Jesus hung on the Cross, why did darkness cover the earth? Because He who knew no sin became sin, so we could be the righteousness of God through Him (Rom. 3:22). What killed Jesus? Jesus could not live apart from the Father. John 6:57 says, "As the living Father hath sent Me so I live by the Father...." Our life was in His blood, but His life was in the Father. Jesus knows the love of the Father (See John 17:26.)

Romans 8:37 says that "we are more than conquerors through Him that loved us." The degree of love that you know determines the degree with which you conquer. That's why we need this love, that's why we've got to have the right heart of love. Remember, we only have one heart, and if you have a problem with one of the people groups in the earth, you ultimately limit God in your life. We need this love because love allows you to conquer.

Love allows you to conquer.

That's why there is a void and a cry in the Muslim people; because when they come to the Father's love, it's over. They will bring a revelation of the Father like never before; because they're the ones who know what it's like to be rejected by a Father. They know what it's like to live in the wilderness for 4,000 years, and then come to a realization of who the Father is.

Then the Muslims will go to the Jewish people and tell them who the Father is. There will be a great revelation of the Father. Many know Jesus, but they don't really know the Father—Jesus said that He came to reveal the Father. That was one of the purposes of Jesus, to reveal the Father.

Matthew 10:19-20 says to take no thought what you must speak in that hour when you come before governments and kings, for not you but the Spirit of my Father shall speak in you. Galatians chapter 4 says that He has given you the Spirit of His Son in your hearts crying Father. Why? The Spirit of His Son cries in your hearts "Abba Father." The Spirit of the Father in your heart reveals the Son. The Spirit of the Father reveals the Son, and the Spirit of the Son reveals the Father.

When you come to Jesus, the Father draws you forth by the Spirit of God. It's about the Father, and Jesus knows that and He came to reveal His Father. When we go to Heaven the Father will ask us one question. What did you do with my son Jesus? And Jesus is going to ask, what did you do with my Father? Do you know my Father, do you know my Father, do you know my Father? Jesus has one cry in His heart—That we will be known of God. He wants us to know His Father.

I believe that Ishmael will come to a revelation of the Father, and he will take it to Israel. And Isaac will break and weep and say I grew up with the Father, I was the one with the covenant, I was the one who was given everything, I was the one through the seed and you were the one who was cast out and rejected and the law cast out—but you've come back with a revelation of the Father. Then Israel will say, "Tell me who the Father is. Tell me how I can know Him."

There is no denying the cry of a human heart. Once the cry is triggered you can't stop it no matter how hard you try. The Spirit of God knows how to get hold of people's hearts. That's why Jesus said, "I'll make you fishers of men." (Mark 1:17). *Men* meaning people's *hearts*, not people's minds. He knows how to bring in *hearts* because He hooks the cry and pulls it in by the Spirit of God.

Ishmael

God blessed Ishmael, but established his covenant with Isaac. Isaac was the child of promise with whom God instituted His covenant for an everlasting covenant, and this included his seed after him.

As a Muslim, I believed that Abraham took Ishmael to the altar of sacrifice instead of Isaac. This is the cornerstone of the Muslim beliefs. The Dome of the Rock sits on the very mount where Abraham took his son. The following presents the truth as it is told in the Bible concerning Ishmael and Isaac. Every Muslim should know what the Bible says about Ishmael and Isaac.

> *And it came to pass after these things that God did tempt Abraham, and said unto him, Abraham: and he said, Behold, here I am. And he said,* ***Take now thy son, thine only son Isaac****, whom thou lovest, and get thee into the land of Moriah; and offer him there for a burnt offering upon one of the mountains which I will tell thee of. And Abraham rose up early in the morning, and saddled his ass, and took two of his young men with him, and Isaac his son, and clave the wood for the burnt offering, and rose up, and went unto the place of which God had told him* (Genesis 22:1-3, emphasis added).

Abraham had already cast out Ishmael with Hagar, leaving him in the wilderness with no inheritance. Ishmael was cast out after Isaac was weaned—when Isaac was no more than three years old. It was several years after Ishmael was cast out when God decided to test Abraham. Ishmael was not even there! Also notice that God deliberately referred to Isaac as Abraham's "only son." After Abraham came closer to the mount, he and Isaac went up alone to worship the Lord.

> *Then on the third day Abraham lifted up his eyes, and saw the place afar off. And Abraham said unto his young men,*

> *Abide ye here with the ass; and **I and the lad** will go yonder and worship, and **come again** to you* (Genesis 22:4-5, emphasis added).

Notice Abraham told the young men he would go with the lad and come back again. He was planning on coming back with Isaac. Abraham believed God would raise Isaac from the dead to fulfill His promise ("*In Isaac shall thy seed be called*") to him.

> *By faith Abraham, when he was tried, offered up Isaac: and he that had received the promises offered up **his only begotten son**, Of whom it was said, That in Isaac shall thy seed be called: Accounting that God was able to raise him up, even from the dead; from whence also he received him in a figure* (Hebrews 11:17-19, emphasis added).

Once again, the Holy Spirit, in the Book of Hebrews, refers to Isaac as Abraham's one and only son. Abraham, by faith, in a figurative sense received Isaac back from the dead. As far as Abraham was concerned, his son was sacrificed unto God and potentially dead. He was serious and took a three-day journey with fire and wood and a knife ready to carry out the sacrifice as an act of obedience.

> *And Abraham took the wood of the burnt offering, and laid it upon Isaac his son; and he took the fire in his hand, and a knife; and they went both of them together. And Isaac spake unto Abraham his father, and said, My father: and he said, Here am I, my son. And he said, Behold the fire and the wood: but where is the lamb for a burnt offering? And*

Abraham said, My son, God will provide himself a lamb for a burnt offering: so they went both of them together (Genesis 22:6-8).

When he answered his son Isaac, Abraham, as a prophet of God, saw into the future and declared that God would Himself provide a lamb. He prophetically spoke of the Lamb of God who would come to take away the sins of the world.

And they came to the place which God had told him of; and Abraham built an altar there, and laid the wood in order, and bound Isaac his son, and laid him on the altar upon the wood. And Abraham stretched forth his hand, and took the knife to slay his son. And the angel of the Lord called unto him out of heaven, and said, Abraham, Abraham: and he said, Here am I. And he said, Lay not thine hand upon the lad, neither do thou any thing unto him: for now I know that thou fearest God, seeing thou hast not withheld thy son, thine only son from me. And Abraham lifted up his eyes, and looked, and behold behind him a ram caught in a thicket by his horns: and Abraham went and took the ram, and offered him up for a burnt offering in the stead of his son (Genesis 22:9-13).

Just before Abraham was about to slay his son, the angel of the Lord called out to him and stopped him. God had provided a ram for Abraham to offer in place of his only son Isaac.

And the angel of the Lord called unto Abraham out of heaven the second time, And said, By myself have I sworn,

> *saith the Lord,* ***for because thou hast done this thing, and hast not withheld thy son, thine only son:*** *That in blessing I will bless thee, and in multiplying I will multiply thy seed as the stars of the heaven, and as the sand which is upon the sea shore; and thy seed shall possess the gate of his enemies; And in thy seed shall all the nations of the earth be blessed; because thou hast obeyed my voice* (Genesis 22:15-18, emphasis added).

Abraham did not withhold his only son Isaac on the mount of sacrifice. For this reason God swore by Himself an oath that, in Isaac, all the nations of the earth would be blessed. Abraham already had the promise, but now he had an oath as an irrefutable guarantee. Ishmael was blessed, but the covenant was made with Isaac, the child of promise, and with his seed after him.

The Seed

God keeps referring to a seed, not all the seeds of Abraham, but to a single seed. This seed that God keeps referring to throughout the Bible was first spoken of in the days of Adam. After the fall of Adam, God prophesied that a Seed of the woman would come forth and bruise the head of satan with His heel. Jesus is the seed of the woman, and He is the seed of Abraham, Isaac, and Jacob. He is the seed of David, and He is the promised seed through which the entire earth is blessed.

...unto us a Son is given...

A Child Is Born but a Son Given

For unto us a child is born, unto us a son is given: and the government shall be upon his shoulder: and his name shall be called Wonderful, Counsellor, The mighty God, The everlasting Father, The Prince of Peace (Isaiah 9:6).

Muslims do not understand how Jesus could be the Son of God. They assume Christians believe that Jesus became the Son of God after being born of the virgin Mary. The Scripture in Isaiah chapter 9 is speaking of Jesus. It says that unto us a child is born, but a Son is given. Jesus was born a child, but He was the Son of God before He ever came to earth and was born of a woman. God gave His only begotten Son. The Son of God was given not born. Jesus is before all things and existed with the Father and was in the Father before all creation.

Who is the image of the invisible God, the firstborn of every creature: For by him were all things created, that are in heaven, and that are in earth, visible and invisible, whether they be thrones, or dominions, or principalities, or powers: all things were created by him, and for him: And he is before all things, and by him all things consist (Colossians 1:15-17).

All things were created by Him and for Him, and through Him alone they exist. **Jesus is the Word of God.** He is the living Word of God.

> *In the beginning was the Word, and the Word was with God, and the Word was God* (John 1:1).

*In the beginning was the Word...*the first part of the verse goes back into eternity when God created all things—that we see and don't see. We know that all things were created by the Word.

*The Word was with God...*the second part of verse goes farther back in time—before anything was ever created, and even then the Word was with God.

*The Word was God...*the third part of the verse goes even farther back when the Word was in God. This is before the Word came out of God.

> *The* ***same*** *was in the beginning with God. All things were made by* ***Him****; and without Him was not any thing made that was made* (John 1:2-3, emphasis added).

In the first part of the third verse, the *Word* is referred to as "Him." Now we begin to see that the Word is a person. This person is Jesus Christ, the Son of God. He is the Word who came out of God, the Word that was with God and the Word by whom all things were created both seen and unseen. He is the image of the invisible God. He is the express image of the Father and the brightness of the glory of God. We are talking about Jesus before He even came to the earth. This person, the Word, came into the world that was made by Him and unto a people to whom He gave light (life) to—but those people did not know Him.

> *That was the true Light, which lighteth every man that cometh into the world. He was in the world, and the world*

> *was made by Him, and the world knew Him not* (John 1:9-10).

This Word then became flesh and took the embodiment of flesh to walk here among us. This Word was born of a virgin and came as a man and lived among us.

> *And the Word was made flesh, and dwelt among us, (and we beheld His glory, the glory as of the only begotten of the Father,) full of grace and truth* (John 1:14).

This Word then revealed unto us the glory of the invisible God. This Word is a person and His name is Jesus Christ.

> *And of his fulness have all we received, and grace for grace. For the law was given by Moses, but grace and truth came by Jesus Christ. No man hath seen God at any time, the only begotten Son, which is in the bosom of the Father, he hath declared him* (John 1:16-18).

Jesus

Jesus is the revelation of the Father, who loves us and sent His Son, Jesus Christ, as the Lamb of God to die for our sins while He Himself was sinless. This same Jesus was crucified, dead, and buried until the third day. Early in the morning of the third day, the Father who sent Him, raised Him from the dead to live forever. This risen Jesus is at the right hand of God in Heaven making intercession for us.

Jesus is real, and when you call on His name, you too will find salvation in Him. He is the living Word and our Savior and Lord.

Jesus is the revelation of the Father.

"Who has ascended up into the heavens or who descended?..." (Prov. 30:4 and John 3:13). This is the question every Muslim and every unbeliever is asking. Jesus is the answer. There is no question in the heart of people that the Scriptures cannot answer—all Scripture is for inspiration by the Spirit of God. When God asks a question, He's not looking for you to answer. He asks so when the answer comes you'll be able to receive it. The Holy Spirit is inspiring the writer and preserving prophetically the questions the human heart ponders in the next text of Scripture.

> *Who hath ascended up into heaven, or descended? who hath gathered the wind in his fists? who hath bound the waters in a garment? who hath established all the ends of the earth? what is His name, and what is his Son's name, if thou canst tell?* (Proverbs 30:4).

This verse asks the questions that every unbeliever, especially Muslims ponder in their hearts. He's asking a question, ***"can you tell me?"*** Can somebody tell me, what is His name, what is His Son's name? How did all creation take place? Who is this One who has ascended and descended, what is His Son's name?

This question is answered in Revelation 19:11-13. The blueprints set forth in the Old Testament also present questions—that are answered in the New Testament through the Holy Spirit. Let's go the Book of Revelation and see the answer:

> *And I saw Heaven opened, and behold a white horse; and He that sat upon him was called Faithful and True, and in righteousness He doth judge and make war. His eyes were as a flame of fire, and on His head were many crowns; and he had a name written , that no man knew, but He Himself. And he was clothed with a vesture dipped in blood: and His name was called the Word of God.* (Revelation 19:11-13).

In Proverbs 30:4, a prophetic question is being asked which is the cry of every human heart. John in his vision is describing Jesus the Son of God who is the Word of God referred to in John 1:1, and here He is clothed with a vesture dipped in blood. His name is called *The Word of God!* What is His Son's name? And He says it's The Word, and His name is Jesus. That's why in Luke 1:31, the angel tells Mary that His name shall be called Jesus.

Jesus is the Hebrew word *Yeshua*, which means "salvation." On the last great day of the feast when Jesus in John chapter 7 says, "if you're thirsty come unto Me and I'll give you drink and cause rivers of living water to flow out of your belly." (Matt. 11:28).

The Jewish people sang, "with joy you will draw water out of the wells of Yeshua."

Then Jesus said something like, "If you're thirsty, let me help you, come to Me. Not only will you get water from my well, but I will cause you to become a well out of which rivers will spring. And not just a well where you have to draw water out, I'm going to cause rivers to come out of your belly. I am Yeshua. I am salvation."

While I'm on the subject of names...John the Baptist, Zechariah's son who was supernaturally conceived in Elizabeth's womb, was named by the angel Gabriel when he came to Zechariah and said you should call his name John. By custom the baby should have been named after his father. Then the angel made Zechariah to be dumb, and he could not speak. Zechariah was not going to be allowed to interfere, because the Seed of the woman was about to come because it was the season. The baby had to be born because he was a forerunner for the Word that was to come.

Jesus said that John came in the spirit and power of *Elijah*. Elijah means "Yahweh is my God." *John* means "Yahweh is gracious." He had to be named John because there was a change in dispensation. For 400 years, there was silence in the earth. They hadn't heard from God; the heavens were closed.

Grace and Salvation

But before you can have *salvation* you must have *grace*, so his name was John so he could say, "Yahweh is gracious"—that was his message. "Repent for the kingdom of Heaven is at hand. Repent of your sins for *He* is coming," John told the people (see Matthew 3:2). John is saying that grace is coming so you can receive Yeshua, who is salvation. That's why salvation is by grace and not by works.

So when a Muslim says salvation is by works; that's what they're missing. There is something about Jesus becoming flesh, about the Word becoming flesh and dwelling among us. Jesus is the Word. That's why you can stand on His Word. He is the Living Word.

Jesus is the Living Word.

Provide Himself a Lamb

The Book of Hebrews says that Abraham's faith was steadfast and that this was the nature of Abraham's faith, this was what God was happy about. He was not only willing to sacrifice his son, he had faith that he would receive his son back from the dead.

At this point in time, Ishmael is not even around, he is out in the wilderness having his own sons. He is married to an Egyptian woman, and God is preserving Ishmael in the wilderness (4,000 years ago). But now here is Isaac, he's at a certain age, and he's about to be sacrificed. It's very important to understand the chronological order: Ishmael has been cast out (he's older than Isaac), and Isaac is now a young man, and the only son Abraham has. God clarified to him and told him that he had to let Ishmael go—even though you love him, you have to let him go. God told Abraham that He will take care of him, and not to worry because He is going to make sure Isaac will be his seed.

Now he's left with Isaac his only son. God comes to him and says it's time to sacrifice him on the altar. That's the end of everything he was promised, that's the end of the promise that "in your seed shall all the families of the earth be blessed."

Abraham walked Isaac to the altar, and in the moment of that test. The Bible says that as he got the knife ready to slay his son; the angel of the Lord spoke from Heaven.

"And Abraham stretched forth his hand and took the knife to slay his son. And the angel of the Lord called unto him out of heaven and said, "Abraham, Abraham..." (Gen. 22:10-11). There it is again, a double annunciation. Was one time not enough? Why does God say his name twice? When He said, "Abraham, Abraham" God was making a statement that He called him Abraham which means "father of many nations," but now it is no longer a promise—God is in the midst of making an establishment. "Abraham, Abraham," father of many nations; the promise is now established in the earth, and it shall not be changed.

"And He said, lay not your hand upon the lad, neither do anything unto him. For now I know you fear God, seeing thou hast not withheld thy son, thine only son from me" (Gen. 22:12). You've not withheld your son, your only son! Why is He calling him his only son? Because he is speaking of a unique son who was born supernaturally of promise.

Isaac was born of a word from Heaven. A word from Heaven that was being fulfilled—the establishment of a prophetic word that "you shall have a son with your wife Sarah, even though she's barren, even though you can't have children." When the Lord met with Abraham, something changed and God told him to go, and by this time next year you will have a son. Not only did Abraham cause a barren womb to become impregnated, after Sarah died Abraham married Katura and had at least six other sons and many other daughters. Abraham had been powerfully anointed—he was eternally changed by the hand of God.

> *And Abraham lifted up his eyes and looked, and behold behind a Ram was caught in a thicket by his horns. And Abraham went and took the Ram and offered him up for a burnt offering instead of his son* (Genesis 22:13).

Why is this Scripture so important? First of all the Old Testament is a blueprint. God sets a blueprint in the natural so that one day when He fulfills it and gives substance in the New Covenant. We can look back to the blueprint and know that it is accurate.

The Word

That's how we know the Word of God is true because the blueprint God has already placed, and it's hidden wisdom no man knows. Only God can begin to reveal it.

For instance, First Corinthians 1 emphasizes how "the Word of God is spiritually discerned." The Word of God is encoded, encrypted.

So when a Muslim comes to me and says something like, "Oh I know the Word of God, and I know everything about the Bible!"

I say politely, "Excuse me, but the Word of God is encrypted and you cannot know the Word apart from the Holy Spirit who teaches spiritual things. Comparing spiritual things with spiritual things, comparing blueprints with substance, He brings them to your heart and He reveals them to your spirit. Your mind can have no argument because it is hidden wisdom that the Spirit of God reveals to the heart of all people."

Meditation Moment

As a Muslim, I believed that Abraham took Ishmael to the altar of sacrifice instead of Isaac, and I was wrong. As a Christian, there may be things that you believe that may not part of God's plan according to His Word. Think about your most foundational beliefs—compare them with God's Word, and allow the Holy Spirit to reveal His wisdom.

Chapter 8

The Confirming Word of God

THERE is hidden wisdom in God's Word. Romans 1:17 says, "the righteousness of God is revealed from faith to faith." It's a revelation of the righteousness of God; it's a revelation of His Word. It's revelation that brings forth faith, that's why the wonderful Scripture says, faith ***comes***. What a powerful statement: "***faith comes*** *by hearing and hearing by the Word of God*" (Rom. 10:17). He didn't say hearing "the Word," He said hearing "by the Word."

The Word is speaking, and it's the Spirit that is the voice of that word, which begins to speak the word and then hidden wisdom is unveiled. Revelation is revealed, and it is concealed in your spirit. You carry the Word in your life. The Word is forever settled in Heaven, but it must be established on earth. In Genesis chapter 22, Abraham, speaking as a prophet in response to his son, declares that "God will provide Himself a lamb for the sacrifice."

In Genesis 22:11 God responds from Heaven with a double annunciation and says, "Abraham, Abraham." Establishing the Word on earth as it is settled in Heaven. Right after this double annunciation God swears by Himself and makes an oath, an irrefutable guarantee, and establishes the promise on earth. It was only a matter of time, and truly Abraham has become the father of many nations.

Now let's go back to Genesis chapter 22 and observe the natural blueprint we have as a result of Abraham's prophetic statement concerning the provision of the lamb in the Old Testament. The prophetic statement in the Old Testament wasn't just for that present time, but it was for our time as well. In the present it was fulfilled; a ram was caught in the thicket, and a lamb was provided. A ram is symbolic of a sacrificial animal, a symbolic bluebrint of the Lamb of God.

Jesus is the Lamb of God.

Abraham was speaking prophetically about a Lamb who would come from Heaven. How do we know this is really true? Abraham couldn't make that statement about the Lamb that God was going to provide unless this statement was already settled in Heaven. The Scriptures tell us that the Lamb of God was slain before the foundations of the world (see Revelation 13:8).

Abraham called the name of that place Jehovah Jireh, and he said, to this day in the mount of the Lord shall be seen,

> *His provision is now seen. And the angel of the Lord called unto to Abraham out of heaven the second time and said by myself have I sworn sayeth the Lord. For because you have done this thing and have not withheld thy only son: That in blessing I will bless you and multiplying I will multiply your* ***seed*** *as the stars of heaven, and as the sand which is upon the seashore and thy seed shall possess the gates of his enemies. And in thy seed shall* ***all the nations*** *of the earth* ***be blessed*** *because thou hast obeyed my voice* (Genesis 22:14-18, emphasis added).

That includes the Muslim people. That includes all of us. Now God made an oath by swearing by Himself. When God makes a promise it is truth because He cannot lie. But He goes one step further, *"by myself I have sworn,"* He swears by Himself, there's nothing else higher to swear by. Because Abraham did not withhold his son from God, all the families of the earth shall be blessed.

This is the second most important question that every Muslim has—because Muslims believe that Abraham offered Ishmael on the altar. The story they believe is almost exactly the same, but they believe it was Ishmael, and not Isaac, who was going to be sacrificed. Their understanding is the "right of the first-born" who is Ishmael because he is the first-born. But we know it is Isaac from reading God's Word.

The Qur'an does not actually mention Isaac's name, but it says "Abraham's son," so they assume it is Ishmael, and that is what they believe. The Qur'an is only 1,400 years old; the Bible is much older in terms of history. Approximately 4,000 years ago is when God made the oath, not just a promise, an oath.

He said, "in thy seed," which is Isaac—that's the key. Why is this important? Because he is the seed through which God would come forth, through which the Word of God would be established in the earth and dwell among us. Then the Word would have to die so as to bear much fruit. That's why the Captain of our salvation desires to bring many sons unto glory. Because He died on the Cross for every person in every nation.

The Cross

Redemption on the Cross is the next statement that Muslims don't believe actually took place.

The same Jesus, who is the Word, became flesh and was crucified on the Cross. Jesus the Word sweats blood in the garden of Gethsemane for the anguish of His soul was so great. Mark 15:25 says, "And it was the third hour, and they crucified Him." It was 9 o'clock in the morning when Jesus was crucified.

This is the Word on a cross. Adam fell short of his glory and lost his crown, He wears a crown of thorns so you and I can wear a crown of glory. The holes in his hands are signs of the covenant of friendship. The holes in His feet provide us shoes to walk in peace—beautiful are the feet of those on the mountains that preach good news. Why the mountains? Because in the mountains there's an echo. Go to the top of the mountains, not one mountain, and say "Jesus!"...it echoes all around. When you speak from a mountain the Voice is heard. That's why we speak from Mount Zion, from a high place, and that's why we preach the gospel—it echoes and shakes the earth.

Shout from the mountaintop.

Jesus the Word was cut and speared on His side. The Muslims think the Cross is foolishness. It is not foolishness; it is the wisdom of God that was hidden until the right time, the right season. Then His plan was revealed, fulfilling a prophetic blueprint concerning the statement Abraham made at the time of the sacrifice of his son Isaac that God will provide Himself a lamb. The Lamb is Jesus.

We're not in the time of "a child was born," we are in "a son was given" time. The Word became the Lamb.

That's why when John saw the vision, he said, "*And He was clothed with a vesture dipped in blood: and His name is called The Word of God*" (Rev. 19:13). There can be no argument who this person is. He is also the Lamb who died on the Cross, and He shed His blood that would remain forever a sign that He is the Lamb of God, He is the Word of God, He is the Son of God who was given to us.

Explain to your Muslim brothers and sisters that the Cross is not foolishness—it is the wisdom of God. Jesus hung on the Cross for six hours, because six is the number of man in the scriptures. Man was created on the sixth day, and Jesus took our Adamic nature to the cross. He became it (the self-nature), and He finished it on the Cross.

Jesus is the Son of God.

Sin and Sin Nature

There is *sin,* and there is *sin nature.* Sin nature abides in every person prior to coming to the saving knowledge of the Cross. When that person receives Christ and is born again the sin nature is stripped away from the spirit of man. The new nature, a divine nature is deposited in their spirit.

Let this thought saturate your heart. This is the same Word, this is Jesus the Word of God who became flesh, who eternally existed in all creation, and all things were made by Him. He was with God, was in God, came out of God, came to earth, dwelt among us, and voiced His Father's thoughts.

This is why I'm a Christian, this is why I believe in Jesus. I don't just believe in the child who was born of a virgin—I believe in the Son who was given as the seed and Word of God. He took on flesh and dwelt among us because He prophetically spoke in Genesis 3:15, that He will send a seed of the woman and He will crush satan's head, and it will cause humankind to be set free. *Now that is the Gospel for a Muslim!*

Muslims are deep, thoughtful people who have a purpose. God has a plan for Ishmael and the Muslim people.

The Blueprint

Why did God meet Hagar through and angel of the Lord in the wilderness when she was pregnant and tell her to "go back to Abraham, go back to your mistress Sarai?" Why was she sent back to Abraham's house? Then, when Ishmael is 15 to 17 years of age, and Isaac was a young child being weaned, God tells Abraham to let Ishmael go. First the Word of the Lord says, "Ishmael, you need to come home." Then the Word of the Lord says, "Ishmael you need to go." Why?

> *For the law, having a shadow of the good things to come, and not the very image of the things, can never with these same sacrifices, which they offer continually year by year, make those who approach perfect* (Hebrews 10:1).

> *for this Hagar is Mount Sinai in Arabia, and corresponds to Jerusalem which now is, and is in bondage with her children* (Galatians 4:25).

God's blueprint in the Old Testament is confirmed in the New Testament concerning the law. Isaac was the son of promise; and when the promise came, the law had to go. When the promised seed, who is the root of David and the seed of Abraham (Jesus in the New Covenant), would come, the Law would go. The Law *leads* you to your need for grace and salvation—Jesus *is* your grace and salvation.

We need to understand the Scriptures. Some people think we don't need the Old Testament. That is incorrect—we need the blueprint! We don't live by the blueprint, but we use the blueprint to build the Kingdom. Now we are building the temple of God on earth, a sanctuary in Heaven. There are three parts to the temple described in First Kings, and there are three parts to us: spirit, soul, and body.

Old Testament blueprint—New Testament truth established! That's why we know the Word of God is true because we have a proven blueprint that tells us the Word of God is true. They're trying to disprove the Word, but they can't because we have a blueprint, and the truth is established in the mouths of two or more witnesses (2 Cor. 13:1).

The Qur'an has no witness; Muslims believe that the Qur'an was revealed to Muhammad by an angel he thought was Gabriel. He described him as Gabriel, but all we know is that an angel of light appeared to him in a cave. And the revelation of the Qur'an came forth.

Muhammad is the only witness saying that the Qur'an is the book from Heaven. On the other hand, the Bible has 40 different witnesses who wrote 66 books that have stood true over thousands of years. All of the writings were composed by the Spirit of God.

Muhammad the only witness.

You can't mess it up even if you tried because you can't understand it without the Holy Spirit revealing it to us. It's the highest encryption in Heaven; you cannot distort it because God reveals it by the Spirit puts it in the New Covenant. He writes the unencrypted Word on our hearts and puts it in our minds—then we know we are His people and that He is our God, and we will declare who He is. The Word is also confirmed by signs and wonders following.

A New Covenant established on even better promises; that's what I'm sharing with you—God will always give Himself a witness. He will fulfill the plans He has for all people using His established blueprints.

The Truth

I hope that this reading is giving you spiritually deep thoughts that prompt you to search yourself to find the Spirit of God resident inside you. I hope you find Christ, the Son of God, and the Spirit of God revealing Himself to you. I pray you find the person of Jesus who redeemed all people as He died on the Cross to prove the Word is true. I pray that you have revelation of the Father sitting on the throne welcoming you to Himself.

The Word of God bears fruit in your life according to His purpose and plan for your life. If it's bearing fruit; that is another witness. The Word is a person and a real relationship. Jesus said the Scriptures testify and reveal Him and are a revelation of a person. That's why Jesus said, "*I AM the truth, I AM the way and I AM the life*" (John 14:6).

For Muslims, the word is not a person, the Qur'an is not a person, it only sits in what they believe is the fourth heaven—they believe there are seven heavens. There is no revelation of a person.

Speak life.

At this point, I'd like to offer a prayer.

Father, I pray for all your precious people, and especially for the one holding this book. I pray that Your Word would become real and that the Living Word will settle into the depths of their being right now. I pray that the deep of their life would call unto the deep of Yours. I pray Lord that all clogging would be removed, and the Rivers of Life would flow freely. I pray that the Holy Spirit will perform surgery and tenderize the soils of your heart so the seed of God can go deeply rooted within you. So when persecution comes and affliction comes for the Word's sake, they shall not be moved.

I speak a shift in the Name of Jesus, a dividing line between soul and spirit and a true embracing of the Spirit of revelation and wisdom, a true embracing of the rivers of life that flow within them, a true embracing of You. And Jesus, I pray that you would become very real to them in every way, every day.

In the name of Jesus I see scales being removed from people's eyes—scales of religion, tradition, and wrong teaching. No matter how you were raised, your spiritual eyes can be opened and flooded with light.

If you have the time right now, please take a moment to close your eyes and let Jesus speak to your heart. Let Him talk to your life and deal with things that are troubling you. Look at the flaming fire in His eyes, allow Him to come and deal with your heart.

Meditation Moment

God's blueprint set forth in the Old Testament gives hope for the future and respect for the past. Is the Word of God planted deeply within your spirit—enough that you can feel His breath and hear His voice? We can make a difference for the Kingdom of God by allowing His love, His sacrifice, and His mercy to flow through us unto those around us. Are you willing?

Chapter 9

Living Epistles

THERE'S a change taking place in the atmosphere of some nations today. I believe that where there has been a famine in the life of His Word, the famine is being removed, and the pure revelation of His Spirit is going to flow. I've seen an open door in the spirit inviting the Church of Jesus Christ to come up higher and see the Word and become the Word on earth. It's an invitation to become living epistles who will be read of all people.

I hope that today's Church will not just hear your Word in the outer court, but they will also walk in the Word in the inner court of their lives.

With the spirit of meekness the Church will receive the engrafted Word that can save souls and come against strongholds. The truth and light of the Word can break traditional thinking and beliefs that hold you back from pursuing God's destiny for you. There's a plumb line descending into your spirit that needs to center on His Word, the Word of God. The plumb line allows you to construct the building so it is straight and upright for a true habitation of God.

When buildings are constructed that are merely structures of people, they are not places in which God dwells. When people build having a revelation of God and follow the plumb line that is centered on Jesus the Word, then the building will stand and God will dwell within it.

I believe we are living in a new era. The way things were done by the churches in the old era, will not work in this one. And what did not work in the old era will work now. This is a season to come before the Lord and say, "Lord, I want to look at your blueprint, not at my own structure to define what you're doing. Give me the blueprint so I can see the substance, so I can have the light. Then I can walk in it, and it can be established."

A door has been opened. Muslims have put their feet down, and they are building mosques in many unlikely places. Spiritual things are being shifted because truth and revelation of His Word is coming forth, and it is breaking something in the atmosphere of nations. There have been things that were "brewing" in the spirit but could not come forth until the right season. That season is drawing nigh and that's why alignment is taking place—that's why shifts and repositioning are occurring in the nation.

Do not be afraid or concerned about the things that are yet to come. But know that the Word that has been spoken to you and revealed to your heart. Know the Word which is His Son Jesus and build a plumb line in your life centered on the Word sown from the Father, which is given by the Father to you. Mindsets will be shifted; patterns and reference points will fall from your minds as strongholds are broken. The limitation of your thinking is being broken in the name of Jesus. What is the next step? Meditate on the Word day and night.

Ishmael's Cry Will Be Heard

God loves the Muslim people. I'm a living example—I was a Muslim. I'm so grateful. All my life, I never imagined or dreamed that I'd know Jesus as the Son of God. As a Muslim, that thought never crossed my mind. I remember walking the streets of Pakistan as a young man, wondering...*Lord, is there even a purpose for my life, any reason I need to live?*

God loves Muslims.

God says in Jeremiah 33:3, "*Call unto me and I will show you great and mighty things you know not.*" The power of life is in the ***"know not"*** realm.

As a Muslim, I knew not who Jesus is, but in the revelation power, one day I did come to know. The future, what you do not know, is where the power lies. It's in that realm of revelation and wisdom where He wants to equip the Church.

That's why Paul prays in Ephesians 3:9, "*that all men see what is the fellowship of the mystery which from the beginning of the world hath been hid in God, who created all things by Jesus Christ.*" I pray that God, the Spirit of wisdom and revelation, will come upon the Church. That the eyes of understanding will be opened and flooded with light. I pray that silent questions will be answered.

I believe there is an entire people group to whom God is revealing Himself and Muslims are part of it. I wasn't seeking after Him. I wasn't consciously searching for Him—but He revealed Himself to me. And I believe that He is going to do the same for millions and millions of people. God told me that a generation of Muslims will come into the Kingdom of God in this season. That is good news!

As living epistles, at some point you will have to address this one particular question.

Who is Jesus and why is He called the Son of God?

Now we know Muslims have a major problem with Jesus being the Son of God. Because I was a Muslim, I can share a Muslim's perspective about what they *think*. Muslims worldwide, when they hear Christians say that Jesus is the Son of God, believe that we are blaspheming Jesus. They believe that a Christian is saying that Jesus, who was born of Mary, became the Son of God because He was born of a virgin.

The Qur'an also says that Jesus was born of a virgin. But what they think Christians are saying is that Jesus was a man who was born of a virgin, then became exalted as the Son of God. They believe that *at that moment* He became the Son of God. That is their understanding and their belief. Muslims also believe that Jesus is a prophet, but not the Son of God. They think that just because He was born of a virgin does not make him the Son of God.

Scriptures help us see the reality of Jesus and how to correctly explain and answer this question that is so deeply rooted in the heart of every Muslim believer. Isaiah 9:6-7 is one of my favorite Scriptures.

> *For unto us a child is born, unto us a Son is given: and the government shall be upon His shoulder: and his name shall be called Wonderful, Counsellor, The mighty God, The everlasting Father, The Prince of Peace. Of the increase of His government and peace there shall be no end, upon the throne of David, and upon His kingdom, to order it, and to establish it with judgment and with justice from henceforth even for ever. The zeal of the Lord of hosts will perform this* (Isaiah 9:6-7).

As explained in the previous chapters, "for unto us a *child is born,* but a *Son is given.*" When Jesus was born of a virgin, a child was *born.* But John tells us that our Father *gave* His only begotten Son.

So Jesus the Son of God pre-existed prior to the virgin birth. That is what Muslims do not understand. They think He showed up *after* He was born of a virgin. What they need to know and understand is that Jesus existed before He appeared on earth and that there is an eternal history and future regarding Jesus.

It is important that we share this aspect of Jesus with Muslims even before sharing the gospel with them. They need to know that "a child is born, but a Son is given." Jesus came and took on the seed of Abraham, and He was conceived in the womb of Mary. It was the Word Himself who was conceived in her womb.

> *Giving thanks unto the Father which has made us able to be partakers of the inheritance of the saints in light. Who hath delivered us from the power of darkness and has translated us into the kingdom of His dear Son: In whom we have redemption through His blood, even the forgiveness of sins. Who is the image of the invisible God, the first born of every creature: For by Him were all things created, that are in Heaven, an that are in earth, visible and invisible, whether they be thrones, or dominions, or principalities, or powers: all things were created by Him, and for Him: And He is before all things, and by Him all things consist* (Colossians 1:12-15).

Everything that was in Heaven was created by Him, and it says, "*and all things are in the earth,*" and then it clarifies it [visible or invisible] "*whether they be thrones, dominions, principalities or powers. All things were created by Him and for Him.*"

This is the same Jesus who was born of a virgin. This is before He was born a child—this is the Son of God. He is before *all* things, there's nothing that He is not before, because He is the source, the root, and the seed. He is the very Word that created ***all*** *things we see and do not see, and by Him all things consist.*

Jesus

Not only is He the source, but He is also the way that things are maintained. That's why it says in the Book of Hebrews that all creation is held up by the Word of His power (speaking of Jesus).

Knowing these things about Jesus will get a Muslim's attention very quickly.

John 3:13 says that "no man hath ascended to Heaven, but He that came down from Heaven, even the Son of man who is in Heaven." Jesus says in John 3:31 that, "he that is of the earth is earthly...[but] He [Jesus] that cometh from Heaven is above all. He is the only one who came from Heaven." That's why John says no one has seen the Father except the Son. No one has seen His shape, no one has seen His form, and no one has known Him except the Son who comes out of the Father, proceeds forth from the Father.

Living epistles please the Father.

Jesus' ministry on the earth was about revealing His Father to us so we could be saved, and save others. Jesus was in contact with the desire of the Father to see us become His children; sons and daughters of God in the family. As living epistles, we should, like Jesus, want to please the Father.

Jesus is the visible of the invisible God. He is the revelation of the Father. Muslims need to know that Jesus is the only one who has come from Heaven—no one has been up to the third Heaven, no one has been to this place in the Father, only Him. Jesus is the only one who has come down to make a way for all of us to arise and get to know Him. We need to show Muslims that there is *eternal history*, and it all begins with Jesus, the Son of God.

Why is it important to identify Jesus as the Word? Because the Qur'an also says that Jesus is the Word of God. It also says that Jesus is the breath of God. So Muslims do believe that Jesus is the Word of God. But they need to understand that all creation was made by the Word, that it was because of the Word that we have life today, things we see and do not see were created by the Word of God.

> *And having come in, the angel said to her, "Rejoice, highly favored one, the Lord is with you; blessed are you among women!" But when she saw him, she was troubled at his saying, and considered what manner of greeting this was. Then the angel said to her, "Do not be afraid, Mary, for you have found favor with God. And behold, you will conceive in your womb and bring forth a Son, and shall call His name JESUS. He will be great, and will be called the Son of the Highest; and the Lord God will give Him the throne of His father David. And He will reign over the house of Jacob forever, and of His kingdom there will be no end." Then Mary said to the angel, "How can this be, since I do not know a man?" And the angel answered and said to her, "The Holy Spirit will come upon you, and the power of the Highest will overshadow you; therefore, also, that Holy One who is to be born will be called the Son of God. ...And Mary said, Behold the handmaid of the Lord; be it unto me according to thy* ***Word****...*(Luke 1:28-35,38).

Notice in John 1:14, "And the Word was made flesh and dwelt among us. And we beheld His glory, the glory as the only begotten of the Father, full of grace and truth."

The same Word by which all things were created, the same Word that was in the beginning and the root of all creation, the same Word that was before that with the Father, the same Word that was in the Father who came out from the Father. Now that same Word is the source of all creation, and has now become flesh and dwelt among us. That's the beginning of the tie of the eternal Word making contact in a person by the name of Jesus on the earth.

Luke chapter 8 says that your Word is your seed. There's a law in the Spirit that says in order for a seed to bear fruit in the earth it must have a body. Every seed that a farmer sows in the ground has a body. Inside the seed there is something that will one day produce life. The seed is sown into the *earth,* which is a blueprint, and then life comes out of that seed.

Today the spirit of the earth in your life is the soil in your heart. He takes the seed of His Word and sows it into your heart. Mary, literally and prophetically, portrays a picture of how the Word is shed abroad and written in our hearts in the New Covenant, because she is the first one to carry this Word in her womb. She was impregnated by the Word of God.

Then a "Child was born" and a "Son was given" to all humankind, because He eternally existed. Now the Word became flesh, and He dwells among us. There is a law, though, that applies—for a seed to bear fruit it must die. No seed in the earth will ever bear fruit until it dies. When a farmer plants a seed in the ground, it has a shell that has to break and die in the soil. Then the life that is in the seed will begin to germinate and emerge from the soil and bears much fruit.

Muslims love revelation and truth, I love this story myself in John chapter 12. "There came certain Greeks among them and came up to worship at the feast. The same came therefore to

Philip which was of Bethesda of Galilee and desired Him saying, sir we would see Jesus."

Jesus says, "The hour has now come that the Son of Man should be glorified." (See John 12:23.) When Jesus turned the water into wine, He said His hour had not yet come. Now He says His hour has come...to go to the Cross.

Why is it time now? Because the Greeks are coming to Him, which is symbolic of the unbelievers. They're knocking on the door—they want to see Jesus! But the only way they're going to see Him, is if He is glorified; when He is crucified.

Jesus says, "*Verily, verily, I say unto you, except a kernel of wheat fall into the ground and die it abides alone, but if it dies it brings forth much fruit*" (John 12:24).

Then He makes a statement by which He's willing to live and die by. "*He that loves his life shall lose it, but he that hates his life in this world shall keep it unto life eternal.*" (See John 12:24-25.) It is key that Jesus begins his comment with "verily, verily" because it signifies that the Word of God is settled in Heaven and the Word of God must be established in earth.

Old Testament Confirmation

Let's see if there's a blueprint for this in the Old Testament because our safety comes from the Old Covenant. Hebrews 10:1 says the New Covenant is the substance of the blueprint which is in the Old Testament.

Several examples of Old Covenant blueprints follow.

Samuel heard a voice but he didn't know it was God talking to him. Samuel talked to his mentor, Eli, a few times and Eli told him that it was the Lord speaking to him. Then when God speaks again, he says, "Samuel, Samuel" and Samuel listens (1 Sam. 3:1-18).

When God calls Abraham, He says, "Abraham, Abraham!" (Gen. 22:11).

When Elisha sees Elijah leave, he says, "my Father, my Father!" (2 Kings 2:12).

Whenever there's a double annunciation in Scripture, it establishes something in the earth that is forever settled in Heaven. In Genesis 41:1-40, Joseph interprets the dream of the Pharaoh. The Pharaoh has two different dreams in the same night, and Joseph gives the interpretation of the dream and says the interpretation of the second dream is the same.

It was doubled so it could be established in the earth. It means it is sure; it shall come to pass. On the basis of that blueprint by the Spirit of God, Jesus says, "Verily, verily, I say unto you." He's making a double annunciation because it establishes something in the earth realm. What is He establishing? "*Except a kernel of wheat fall into the ground and die, it abides alone.*" He's talking about Himself.

The Bible says in Luke chapter 8 that Jesus is the Seed, and He is the Word of God, which is the seed of God. He came to the earth.

Mark chapter 4 says that the sower soweth the Word. Jesus never made a statement that was not true of Himself and the Father because what He said He heard of the Father. And the Father Himself does not speak something that is not in line with the ways of God. The Father is the first Sower of all time, He is the first One who sowed the Word. Therefore Jesus called us to be sowers of the Word—to be living epistles.

But here's the Word that the Father has sown, and in order for the Word or a seed to be truly sown and to bear fruit, it must die. Every seed has a body given by God, and Jesus the Word became flesh and took on a body and walked among us. That's why the Scripture says, God prepared a body for Jesus for sacrifice. (See Hebrews 10:5.) So Jesus the Word is delivered from Mary as a baby with a body destined to be sacrificed. He grew to adulthood. He died on the Cross, and He was buried. His body was broken. The shell of the seed was broken, and He dies because He knows that unless the seed dies and falls to ground it abides alone. (See John12:24.) That is why the shell of a seed dies for life to germinate out of it.

As a living epistle, if you share all these things with a Muslim, about now the Muslim mind is probably wondering, *what is going on?* Because they understand truth for the first time, and their heart will be drawn toward the Word, because they're willing to live and die by the Word.

Jesus had the right to die.

Jesus the Seed died for three days, but there is something even more powerful in the death of Jesus on the Cross. Because He is the root of all creation, He was the only One who has the right to die on behalf of all creation. Not just for the redemption of humankind, but as the Scriptures say, one day even the earth itself will be redeemed into a new Heaven and a new earth. All corruption will be removed.

First Corinthians 15 speaking of the natural body says the seed is sown in corruption, but it is raised in incorruption. That's what happens to a seed when it's planted in the ground. Same thing with Jesus; He accepted our sin on the Cross. He became sin, became corruption, He who knew no sin—so you and I could be the righteousness of God in Him. On the Cross He died, shed His blood, and three days later God raised Him from the dead. And the same Word is now available to dwell in the hearts of all people.

> ***God who at sundry times and in diverse manners*** [many different ways] ***spoke in times past unto the fathers by the prophets,*** *Hath in these last days spoken unto us by His Son whom He has appointed heir of all things, by whom also He made the worlds* (Hebrews 1:1-2 KJV, emphasis added).

The Word made all the worlds, made all creations, and He is an heir. First, He's the source of all creation, and now He's an heir who's going to reap all as an inheritance. It says in these last days He's spoken by His son. Why? Because Jesus the Word rose from the dead and now dwells in all hearts—and God speaks through Jesus. In the Old Testament He spoke through the prophets to prophesy and laid a blueprint; now He speaks through Jesus to us.

Hear the Word, See the Son

We're moving into an era when the Word shall not just be heard, but the Son shall be seen. The West and secular society has soothed the Church by acknowledging the child who was born in the manger in an effort to deny the reality of the Son of God who was given. They have tried to keep Him only a baby in a manger. They acknowledge the baby in the manger, but at the same time they deny the Son of God! They do not acknowledge that the baby who was born is the Son that was given to save all humankind for the sins of the world—the only begotten Son of God, that whosoever should believe upon Him shall have eternal life (see John 3:16). We have heard of the child who was born, but now it's time to see the Son who was given. Let's continue our study and look into Genesis 3:9-15.

> *And the Lord God called unto Adam, and said unto him, Where art thou? And he said, I heard thy voice in the garden, and I was afraid, because I was naked; and I hid myself. And he said, Who told thee that thou wast naked? Hast thou eaten of the tree, whereof I commanded thee that thou shouldest not eat?*
>
> *And the man said, The woman whom thou gavest to be with me, she gave me of the tree, and I did eat. And the Lord God said unto the woman, What is this that thou hast done? And the woman said, The serpent beguiled me, and I did eat.*
>
> *And the Lord God said unto the serpent, Because thou hast done this, thou art cursed above all cattle, and above every beast of the field; upon thy belly shalt thou go, and dust shalt thou eat all the days of thy life:*
>
> *And I will put enmity between thee and the woman, and between thy seed and her seed; it shall bruise thy head, and thou shalt bruise his heel* (Genesis 3:9-15).

This first prophetic word then being released is intended to affect the realm of time forever. In this word He is giving in Genesis, He is also making a promise. He says He will put enmity between the woman and the serpent. Why is He talking to the serpent like that? Because satan did not have jurisdiction in the realm of earth at this time because he had been banished.

God gave man dominion over the works of His hand and He gave Adam a seat of authority. The enemy was after Adam's seat of authority so he could be the (small "g") god of this world, second heaven down. In order to communicate with Adam he convinced the serpent to allow him to use his body. So God is not just speaking of the serpent, He's speaking of him who laid hold of that body of the serpent, satan, and said there will be enmity between the devil and the woman. That's why the enemy hates women!

But God also makes a prophecy to the woman. He tells her that she will have travailing in childbirth when the seed comes forth. But a seed is going to come forth from her, through a virgin, through the womb of a woman, who will bruise satan. God says that the day will come when the Seed will come, born through the woman whom you have deceived, who will remain pure and will bruise you. This Seed will take back the authority satan took from Adam! This Seed will bruise satan's head, bruise his authority, rob him, spoil, and shame him openly.

Jesus the Seed.

Jesus the Seed will redeem man and be exalted to the highest seat in the heavens and the earth on the right hand of the Father.

He will cause us to be seated with Him in Christ, far above satan! God is telling satan in Genesis that when Jesus comes, the Word who becomes flesh, He has the authority to bruise the heel of satan, who caused a separation between humanity and God.

That's why satan carefully kept an eye on everyone who was born. That's why satan inspired Cain with evil intentions to kill his brother, Abel, thinking he could destroy the seed of God! Eight generations later, Noah showed up.

I believe that Genesis chapter 6 says that fallen angels looked upon women who were fair and had children with them and this perverted the seed in the earth. "*The Lord said, My spirit shall not always strive with man, for that he also is flesh...*(Gen. 6:3). God's heart is grieved and He flushed out all the perversion with a worldwide flood. But He spared Noah and the eight members of his family. He preserved the seed that would one day come forth. His Word and seed would not come through perversion, it would come forth through righteousness as a result of a faithful person such as Noah, a preacher of righteousness.

Eight generations later, there is Abraham. God tells him that He will make Abraham a great nation and will bless him and make his name great and that he shall be a blessing. That sounds great to Abraham, but the next verse in Genesis chapter 12 says, "*I will bless them that bless you and curse them that curse you and in thee shall all the families of the earth be blessed.*" God tells Abraham that his seed will produce a great nation. God says the same thing about the seed to Isaac and Jacob. The seed God is referring to is that of the woman who is going to crush satan's head.

There is a history in all of Scripture. Why is this so important for a Muslim? Because the Muslim is told in the Qur'an that there are four books that came from Heaven. The first is the Holy Bible. The second speaks of the Psalms of David, which I will refer to later, the third refers to the New Testament or the book that came as a result of Jesus. The fourth book is the Qur'an.

The Qur'an says to "have faith equally in all the books." So it is the responsibility of every Muslim to know about the other three books before the Qur'an. Every Muslim has a right to know what is written in these other three books.

Preserving the Seed

Through Abraham God makes a distinction about who He's going to make His covenant with, and He says His covenant shall be with Isaac. He blessed Ishmael and preserved him for a season because God is going to use him in the endtimes. But—God's seed through which the whole earth is going to be blessed came through Abraham to Isaac and Jacob.

God separated Abraham from the nations unto Himself. He separated Isaac from Ishmael, and He separated Jacob from Esau because He was preserving the lineage of the seed—so the Seed would be established on the earth. Now we go back to John 1:14 and understand that the Son given is the Word that became flesh and dwelt among us. That's why Jesus is called the Word of God.

One day during our time, all things will be connected—all questions answered. Glory be to God.

Meditation Moment

Jesus is the answer to every question. Are the churches ready to provide His answer to those asking the tough questions? Are the churches ready to open their hearts to His plan for the Muslims and unbelievers? Directing our prayers to connect all people to the Kingdom of God will provide the answers to the questions that the world is asking.

Chapter 10

Muslim Wealth and Ishmael's Blessing

I believe that the Holy Spirit is speaking to leaders in the Body of Christ concerning wealth and finances for Kingdom purposes. Many have a keen sense that a great transfer of wealth is coming to the Church to transact Kingdom business. I believe God is giving men and women unconventional ideas about ministry and finances in the 21st century.

God is raising up apostles and prophets in these last days who will have their own oil wells to deliver the Word of the Lord. They will have the financial resources to establish God's covenant on the earth. God will give creative ideas to the Body of Christ that will position believers in places of financial dominion in times of famine in the world. There will be a dominion anointing to function in the marketplace that will marvel skeptics in the business world. God is about to bring many into a wealthy place so they can fund the greatest harvest ever.

God is not going to place the command of such wealth into the hands of people who do not know their purpose in the Kingdom. It is necessary to know the purpose for which you were created and to recognize the gift that is within you to fulfill your destiny. Revelation of purpose precedes the manifestation of provision.

When we know our destined purpose, an uncompromising passion is born. Divine purpose gives birth to authentic passion which, in turn, stirs up the gift of God within us. *When the gift within us is stirred, it always brings prosperity to accomplish the God-given purpose in our lives, leaving more than enough to help finance other God-given ideas in the Kingdom.* God sent us into the world not to accumulate money, but to glorify God and serve one another in love. Money is merely a tool that can be used for good or bad; it takes on the nature of the person it is entrusted to.

We must understand our purpose from a Kingdom perspective. A Kingdom mentality realizes that our God-given purpose is to enhance the Kingdom of God and not our own kingdom or agenda. A Kingdom mentality is about stewardship rather than ownership. We are merely stewards of the resources entrusted to us to establish His covenant. In the Kingdom, we own nothing yet partake of everything that God has in Christ.

> *But thou shalt remember the Lord thy God: for it is he that giveth thee power to get wealth, that he may establish his covenant which he sware unto thy fathers, as it is this day* (Deuteronomy 8:18).

God gives us the power to get wealth, but we must not forget that it is for the purpose of establishing His covenant on the earth. This is the same covenant that God made with Abraham to bless all the families of the earth through his seed whom we know as the Lord Jesus Christ.

We establish the covenant by fulfilling the destiny for which we were created and placed on this earth. We can only establish His covenant on the earth by specifically doing that which we were destined to do. The purpose of God is in us, and every purpose of God is redemptive in nature and will directly or indirectly advance the Gospel.

Some may be called to the five-fold ministry, while others are called to establish television stations and satellites as a medium to proclaim the Gospel. Someone designs, another engineers, and yet another manufactures technology for our everyday use. Of course, television is not dedicated solely to the use of God; in a fallen world, neither are computers, radio, Internet, airplanes, automobiles, and so on.

Establish God's promise
by fulfilling your destiny.

We cannot limit our thinking when establishing our destiny in the earth for His Kingdom. Although we are living in the world, we are not of the world (John 15:19). Let us be established in our understanding that the power to get wealth goes hand-in-hand with the purpose for which we are destined on this earth—for His glory. Why give up everything to the devil and allow him to use what is meant for the Kingdom of God?

God's Purpose in Blessing Ishmael

We know God's works are clothed with purpose. God's provision is always hidden in His blessing. I would like to share with you the role of Ishmael in the end-time wealth transfer:

> *And as for Ishmael, I have heard thee: Behold, I have blessed him, and will make him fruitful, and will multiply him exceedingly; twelve princes shall he beget, and I will make him a great nation* (Genesis 17:20).

Ishmael was deprived of the blessing of Abraham and any inheritance when he was cast out in the wilderness with his mother Hagar. But God did bless Ishmael with an unconditional blessing; and as a result, this blessing has accumulated and wealth has been stored up in the Muslim world. As you read previously, the Middle East alone provides more than half of the world's oil.

For years, Ishmael's oil wells have been storing up wealth in the Muslim world that has spilled into the commerce and the business communities worldwide. They are very careful to support other Muslim businesses first, much like the Jewish communities. Muslims are forbidden in the Qur'an to charge interest, and Muslim lending organizations do not charge interest to other Muslims on mortgages and loans. This way, their homes are paid off more quickly. They accumulate more equity in their homes, and they can invest in more property.

They also believe in owning land, property, and real estate wherever they settle. The Muslim people have been zealous about both their religious and their economic dominions. There is an enormous amount of wealth that has been stored up for thousands of years in the Muslim world, and it is still being stored up today. From the earliest days on, the Ishmaelites were businessmen who traded in the marketplace with caravans of goods. Commerce was a way of life for them. This wealth has been stored up for a purpose.

> Provision for His purpose
> is hidden in His blessing.

God blessed Ishmael thousands of years ago, knowing that when he would come into the Kingdom, the treasure hidden in dark places and the secret treasure that is stored up will come into the Kingdom, to finance the Gospel in part. Even the oil in the wells will be for the Gospel's sake. He has provision for His purpose hidden in His blessing.

I believe that God blessed Ishmael unconditionally with the intention to fund the end-time harvest in part. We will see enormous wealth transfer from the Muslim world in the billions and trillions. God preserved the oil and raw materials in the earth for resources to establish His covenant. He created the earth in its fullness and all that is in the earth belongs to Him. God gives the power to get wealth for the sole purpose of establishing His covenant. God blessed Ishmael for the establishment of His covenant in the endtimes.

The Glory and the Gold

The Church has been concerned about the oil in the Middle East and the financial backing of Islam. In the meantime, we have taken for granted the oil of the Spirit that we possess. Ishmael longs to be refreshed with fresh oil from Heaven. There is going to be an exchange of oil in these last days. The oil in the Middle East will be exchanged for the oil in the Kingdom of God. God desires to bring the streams of oil together. Wealth and substance coming into the Kingdom is not foreign. There is insight in the Word of God:

> *Arise, shine; for thy light is come, and the glory of the Lord is risen upon thee. For, behold, the darkness shall cover the earth, and gross darkness the people: but the Lord shall arise upon thee, and his glory shall be seen upon thee. And the Gentiles shall come to thy light, and kings to the brightness of thy rising* (Isaiah 60:1-3).

As we study the Scriptures, we see the glory of God coming upon the Church and the manifestation of His glory causing nations and kings to come into the Kingdom.

> *Then thou shalt see, and flow together, and thine heart shall fear, and be enlarged; because the abundance of the sea shall be converted unto thee, the forces of the Gentiles shall come unto thee. The multitude of camels shall cover thee, the dromedaries of Midian and Ephah; all they from Sheba shall come: they shall bring gold and incense; and they shall shew forth the praises of the Lord. All the flocks of Kedar shall be gathered together unto thee, the rams of Nebaioth shall minister unto thee: they shall come up with acceptance on mine altar, and I will glorify the house of my glory* (Isaiah 60:5-7).

According to Scripture, the wealth and treasure of the Gentiles will come into the Kingdom. Muslims represent 42 percent of the Gentiles today. In verses 6 and 7, we see a description of the forces of the Gentiles that will come into our hands. Kedar was the second son of Ishmael and ancestor to Mohammed, the prophet of Islam. The Scripture says that all the flocks of Kedar, speaking of the people and the wealth and substance of Ishmael, will transfer into the Kingdom. Muslims have always directed their wealth toward their religious beliefs—the expansion of Islam through the building of mosques and so on. When their eyes are opened, they will catch the vision of God's heart and continue to passionately support the Gospel. I believe that when Ishmael is revived in the presence of God, he will lay his treasures at the feet of Jesus and embrace his destiny.

From Terrorism

Among the Muslim people, as we have discussed, are those who have embraced the spirit of Esau in the face of terrorism, and they are funding terrorism with their accumulated wealth. Billions of dollars go into terrorism, weapons, and training—and to the families of suicide bombers in recognition of their deeds. The spirit of Esau has abused part of the wealth of Ishmael. As God judges the spirit of Esau and answers the cry of Ishmael, the flow of money will be directed into the Gospel. As light comes forth concerning the destiny of Ishmael and the purpose of his blessing, then the wealth transfer will occur in its fullness. Revelation of purpose always exceeds the manifestation of provision.

Muslim wealth has been transferred from generation to generation. In this last generation, there will be a movement of God that will bring the inherited wealth into the Kingdom.

Marketplace Transactions

God will cause men in business to rise up; and He will give them wisdom and witty inventions to transact great wealth with the Muslim countries. God is raising up people who will have cutting-edge market ideas for the Muslim world. This movement of God will touch Muslim billionaires and open their eyes to the divine purpose behind their blessing. God will connect these people with Kingdom business people, and great wealth will be transacted. To the everyday world, it will be business as usual, but in reality, it will be a strategic business plan for the Kingdom of God.

Hidden Treasures

> *And I will give thee the treasures of darkness, and hidden riches of secret places, that thou mayest know that I, the Lord, which call thee by thy name, am the God of Israel* (Isaiah 45:3).

There is more than enough hidden wealth in the world to finance the Gospel worldwide a million times over. It is just a matter of who possesses that wealth. Wealth can either change hands or the people who hold it can change. Either way, it will be used to establish the covenant of God. Our God, in His wisdom, has always intended to pay for His purposes through the blessing He empowers us with. *The blessing* is a spiritual endowment. But blessings are a natural result of that spiritual empowerment of a person.

God blessed Abraham to be a blessing to the entire world in Christ Jesus. Likewise, God blessed Ishmael, knowing that one day he would finance the Gospel in part. That wealth has been stored up for generations and now will be released into the Kingdom. Provision favors the blessed.

Provision favors the blessed.

Unity

Divine purposes are always bigger than one person. No purpose of God is meant to be accomplished alone. Even Jesus did not fulfill the will of God alone. What we are destined to do will not be accomplished apart from divine relationships in the Kingdom. The Body of Christ is comprised of believers, and every member of the Body has an important function. When we come together, our comprehension of the purposes of God is synergized, and our understanding is fruitful.

Unity creates a platform for a commanded blessing (see Psalm 133). Unity merges individual destiny with corporate destiny. Corporate destiny brings greater revelation concerning the purposes of God and puts a greater demand on the anointing to get wealth in order to establish His covenant. A body has many parts, and each part has its unique function. Every part is needed in order for the body to function in its fullness.

The Body of Christ is the same; we must work together. New wine is always found in a cluster of grapes, and that is where the blessing is (see Isaiah 65:8). A grape apart from the cluster is not much good for wine, and neither is a believer apart from the Body. Unity is the breeding ground for unlimited potential beyond what we can ask or think, according to the power that works in us (see Ephesians 3:20). Unity creates within us the capacity to withstand and utilize greater measures of wealth transfer in order to establish the covenant of God.

Let us ensure that our hearts are united in purpose for the greatest wealth transfer ever seen. I believe God blessed Ishmael, not in vain, but for the Gospel's sake in this hour.

Meditation Moment

"For the love of money is the root of all evil" (1 Tim. 6:10). Today's Western society is consumed with a get-rich-quick mentality. The "bottom line" and the "next big deal" keeps business and political minds churning. From the decadence of the oil-rich Middle East to the suffering poor of African nations, where do you and I fit in?

Chapter 11

Gather Your Nets for the Harvest

ALL nations come from one blood and are saved by the blood of One, Jesus Christ. Man divides, but God separates unto Himself. Noah replenished the earth after the flood, and from 70 nations, God separated unto Himself a people through Abraham, Isaac, and Jacob, who became Israel.

God, throughout the Old Testament, recognized two groups of people, Jews and Gentiles. God blessed all the nations of the earth in Christ Jesus, giving birth to the Church: one new man made of Jew and Gentile alike in faith in Jesus, the Messiah. God loves these three groups of people: Jews, Gentiles, the Church, and is working out His plan for them (see 1 Corinthians 10:32).

The Harvest

The harvest is ready for reaping. Men and women have gone out to the nations and given their lives for the cause of the Gospel. Many who have been martyred for Jesus we may never hear about this side of Heaven. But their blood is not forgotten, nor is their labor of love in vain; including missionaries today who have spent all their lives ministering to Muslims and have not seen the fruit they would like to see. It seems they have toiled all night and have caught no fish.

I believe as you read the following Scriptures you will be encouraged in the Lord. Let me share with you a prophetic picture of the times in which we are now living, concerning the harvest:

> *After these things Jesus showed himself again to the disciples at the sea of Tiberias; and on this wise showed he himself. There were together Simon Peter, and Thomas called Didymus, and Nathanael of Cana in Galilee, and the sons of Zebedee, and two other of his disciples.*
>
> *Simon Peter saith unto them, I go a-fishing. They say unto him, We also go with thee. They went forth, and entered into a ship immediately; and that night they caught nothing.*
>
> *But when the morning was now come, Jesus stood on the shore: but the disciples knew not that it was Jesus. Then Jesus saith unto them, Children, have ye any meat? They answered him, No. And he said unto them, Cast the net on the right side of the ship, and ye shall find. They cast*

> *therefore, and now they were not able to draw it for the multitude of fishes....*
>
> *And the other disciples came in a little ship; (for they were not far from land, but as it were two hundred cubits,) dragging the net with fishes. As soon then as they were come to land, they saw a fire of coals there, and fish laid thereon, and bread.*
>
> *Jesus saith unto them, Bring of the fish which ye have now caught. Simon Peter went up, and drew the net to land full of great fishes, an hundred and fifty and three: and for all there were so many, yet was not the net broken. Jesus saith unto them, Come and dine...* (John 21:1-12).

Jesus has always desired for us to be fishers of people. He told His disciples He would make them fishers of men. Just like the disciples of Jesus, the Church has been out fishing for generations in the sea of humanity. We even have "ships," speaking of the tools and equipment with which we preach the Gospel, while fishing in the sea of humanity. Yet many have fished through the night and feel like they have caught no fish.

Maybe you have worked all night in the Muslim mission field and have not seen the results you have desired. Imagine, it is the early morning hour, and Jesus is standing at the shore and maybe you have been unable to recognize Him. But He is telling you to cast your nets on the right side of the ship.

Cast your nets again.

I believe we have entered the dawn of a supernatural harvest. We are alive in the dawning of a *kairos* moment and experiencing the beginning of a different season. Jesus is asking the Church to cast her nets on the right side of the ship, for He is about to fill her nets with the harvest of multitudes.

There will be a supernatural harvest of Muslims and the nations of the world into the Kingdom. We have been fishing with poles, but Jesus is telling us to cast our nets on the right side of the ship. *It is time to move from poles to nets.* It is time to move from *our* vision to *His* vision for the Kingdom. Our vision must expand to encompass the greater purpose of God being worked out in the earth. Corporate vision always enhances personal vision and allows for maximum impact in the Kingdom. Let us look beyond our fishing poles into the face of Jesus and obey His command to cast the net.

I believe today's nets are television, media, satellite, Internet, radio, and unconventional ideas. I believe Jesus is giving unconventional instructions to ministries coming forth in this hour. Jesus has been speaking to ministries and churches to unite and form unconventional nets for the harvest. For 2,000 years, Jesus has taught believers how to be fishers, but now He is standing at the shore, causing the fish to flow into our nets, making us fishers of multitudes. We must move from a fisher*man* mentality to a fisher-*multitude* mentality. Some of us will have to put away our fishing poles and gather up nets for this hour.

God will use nets in this season to harvest the Muslim people in particular. The wall of Islam has fallen, and the gates are now open for the Gospel to go forth. The time has come for them to come into the Kingdom. We are about to witness a miraculous harvest of souls. Jesus is standing at the shore, calling out to the Church with a command to cast the nets on the right side of the ship. We must obey His command.

The disciples obeyed Him and cast the net on the right side of the ship, and they could not draw the net in because of the quantity of fish. Likewise, we are about to see a supernatural harvest of the multitudes such that we will not be able to contain them in our churches today. This harvest will be so great that we will have to call upon all our brethren to help draw the nets and carry the harvest to shore. Jesus waits at the shore for us and desires for us to bring the harvest to Him.

Gather your nets!

You Are Invited

The invitation is open for all of us to come to Him. But before we rush to dine with Him, let us obey the command and cast the net and gather the harvest and bring it to Jesus. Then we can all dine as much and as long as we want to. How could we possibly leave such a multitude of fish in the sea with Jesus at the shore?

There is a fresh anointing being released upon men and women in the Church for a supernatural harvest. Cast the net on the right side of the ship, for a multitude awaits your decision. Be not afraid; the net will not break, and an overflow of the harvest will come in. The Scripture specifically records that they caught 153 large fish. I believe this specific number speaks to us beyond a mere quantity of fish. *One* is the number of preeminence in the Bible, *five* is the number of grace, and *three* is the number of divine perfection. There is a preeminent grace of divine perfection being made manifest for this supernatural harvest of the multitudes. Jesus is standing at the shore. You may not be able to see Him, but can you hear Him?

The Coming of the Lord Is Near

> *Be patient therefore, brethren, unto the coming of the Lord. Behold, the husbandman waiteth for the precious fruit of the earth, and hath long patience for it, until he receive the early and latter rain. Be ye also patient; stablish your hearts: for the coming of the Lord draweth nigh* (James 5:7-8).

Israel awaits the coming of the Messiah; Muslims await the return of Jesus, and the Church is anticipating the soon-coming King. The world is watching the end-time events, and there is great anticipation for the closing of the age. The return of the Lord Jesus is drawing nigh, but God is waiting for the precious fruit of the earth. His eyes are on the harvest, while our eyes are on the clock.

A new season is making way for the rains of Heaven to fall upon the harvest fields of the earth. "*The Lord is...not willing that any should perish, but that all should come to repentance*" (2 Peter 3:9). He is calling us, His Church, to divinely cooperate with His grace that is flowing for the nations today, in particular the Islamic nations. Will we cooperate?

Meditation Moment

What if you don't know any Muslims? What if the majority of your community and workplace colleagues are Christian neighbors and friends—are you willing to reach out beyond your comfort zone to share the Gospel? Is there a way you can encourage your Church to see Jesus standing on the shore and to help cast nets on the other side of tradition? Seek God's face concerning the new and different ideas presented. Pray that "*none shall perish.*"

Concluding Thoughts

THE primary intent of this book is to define and clarify the season we are in, and to bring understanding and create awareness of the significance of Ishmael and his role in provoking Israel to salvation.

However, the full intent of this book is to testify of God's mercy and provision, so none will perish and all will come to repentance. In many ways, this book serves to provoke us to think outside of our comfort boxes and embrace God's plan for salvation of the nations of the earth. It is a testimony to the truth that the earth will be filled with the knowledge of the glory of our God.

Will we be like the sons of Issachar and discern this season (see 1 Chronicles 12:32)? If we do, our walk will be graced with wisdom and empowered by revelation, partnering with Heaven, to see the greatest harvest yet seen.

Embrace the prophetic truth revealed in this book as a forerunner of something mightier yet to come!

Concluding Thoughts

Prayer to Know God

IN reading this book, the desire in your heart to know God as Father may have stirred deeply within you. Maybe you would like to genuinely experience His love, forgiveness, and acceptance.

God desires to open your eyes and show you the specific purpose for which you were designed. Destiny within you is longing to be unlocked by truth in the person of Jesus. If you would like to begin a relationship with God, say this prayer out loud in your own words:

> *Dear Heavenly Father, You are the Most High God, and I come to You in the name of Jesus. I thank you for sending Jesus to the earth as the Word of God who became flesh. Father, I receive Your love and gift of salvation in the person of Jesus Christ.*
>
> *Jesus, I believe You died on a cross and shed Your blood for my sins and the sins of the whole world. I believe God raised You from the dead on the third day. Jesus, come into my heart. Take away my stony heart and give me a new heart that I may love the Father even as You do.*

If you prayed this prayer, please contact us at:

Covenant of Life Ministries
PO Box 27055
Lethbridge, AB T1K 6Z8
E-mail: info@covenantoflife.org
Website: www.covenantoflife.org

My Prayer for You

Father, I thank You in the name of Jesus that Your Spirit will witness with my brother or sister that they are children of God. Father, make known to them Your ways and show them Your covenant. Manifest your presence and touch them deeply with your Holy Spirit and unveil your Word to them continually.

Amen.